i ♥ pies and tarts

i ♥ pies and tarts

NANCY KERSHNER

taylor trade publishing

Lanham ♥ New York ♥ Dallas ♥ Boulder ♥ Toronto ♥ Oxford

Published by Taylor Trade Publishing
An imprint of The Rowman & Littlefield Publishing Group, Inc.
4501 Forbes Boulevard, Suite 200
Lanham, Maryland 20706

Distributed by National Book Network

Interior design by Piper E. Furbush

Library of Congress Cataloging-in-Publication Data

Kershner, Nancy, 1965–
    I love pies and tarts / Nancy Kershner.—1st ed.
        p. cm.
    Includes index.
    ISBN 1-58979-249-1 (pbk. : alk. paper)
    1. Pies   I. Title.
    TX773.K463 2005
    641.8'652—dc22   2005003528

contents

INTRODUCTION	vi
GETTING STARTED	1
ALL-AMERICAN FRUIT PIES	13
TRADITIONAL FAVORITES	31
CHOCOLATE PIES	53
RUSTIC DESSERTS	71
SOPHISTICATED TARTS	91
SAVORY PIES	107
INDEX	117

"As American as apple pie." Like baseball and hot dogs, pies are quintessentially American. Since revolutionary soldiers first encountered this convenient and delicious method of cooking—sandwiching a filling between two crusts—in the Pennsylvania Dutch countryside, pie making has spread across the country and come to represent hospitality, generosity, and welcome.

I ♥ Pies and Tarts started with my grandmother's recipe for apple dumplings. Wrapping the tart dough around cored apples stuffed with nuts and raisins, she baked individual little pies and served them warm, sitting in a pool of cold milk. After a decade as a pastry chef, training in France and Italy and creating pastry menus for New York's hottest restaurants, I have gathered inspiration and recipes for this collection of modern pies and tarts from all over.

I ♥ Pies and Tarts is a short but definitive guide to creating luscious, modern, one-dish desserts—and a few entrées—in the time-honored traditions of American pie making. Recipes in this book range from rustic pies of the Pennsylvania Dutch countryside, such as Amish Vanilla Pie and Pennsylvania Dutch Apple Dumplings, to sophisticated and modern European-inspired tarts, including Apricot Frangipane Tart and Lemon Curd Tartlets. Traditional favorites and new modern classics from across the country helped inspire this collection of over fifty recipes for tarts and pies, as well as a chapter of basic dough recipes. Additional information is offered regarding serving suggestions, alternative ingredients, time-saving products, and tips for adjusting the pies to special dietary restrictions. From the country roadside Farm Stand Apple Pie to the elegant Double Chocolate Ganache Tarts, *I ♥ Pies and Tarts* provides simple instructions and basic explanations that result in beautiful tarts and pies.

The recipes begin with the pies that started the tradition of pie making, the all-American fruit pies. These pies include blueberry, peach, apple, and sour cherry. Each recipe focuses on a different fruit or fruit combination and explains how to prepare that filling. The next section presents traditional favorites, with recipes for holiday pies as well as the classic pies that regularly turn up at your favorite restaurant. These pies include Toasted Coconut Custard, Mile-High Lemon Meringue, and Bourbon Pecan Pie.

Because chocolate is one of the few foods that inspires even more passion than pie, an entire section is dedicated to chocolate pies. You'll find recipes for French Silk Pie with Raspberries, Chocolate Cream Cheese Peaks, and Frozen Peanut Butter Mousse Pie.

A section on rustic pies covers crustless pies, which are little more than fruit wrapped in dough, and individual everyday snack pies. Some recipes in this section include Individual Fig Crostatas, Individual Apricot Cherry Fried Pies, and Deep-Dish Plum Cobbler.

For a change of taste, the next section contains the elegant and refined straight-sided tart. With precise and dramatic presentations, such tarts as the French Clafoutis Cherry Custard Tart, Walnut Caramel Tart, and the elegant Fresh Berry Tart will delight the eye and the palate.

The final section of recipes explores the world of pies as most of the world recognizes pie, that is, the savory pie. Greek Spinach Feta Pie, Quiche Lorraine, and English Steak and Kidney Pie help round out the chapter.

As pie making moves into a more modern era, time-stressed households have lost some of the traditions passed from generation to generation. By providing quick and convenient methods of producing the pies and tarts that define an American tradition, *I ♥ Pies and Tarts* brings back your great-grandmother's recipes and introduces the sophisticated flavors and presentations of baking today.

notes

getting started

PERFECT PIE DOUGH   4

CREAM CHEESE PIE DOUGH   6

COOKIE CRUST   7

SWEET TART DOUGH   8

NO-ROLL PIE DOUGH   9

SAVORY TART DOUGH   10

The secret to a great pie is fresh ingredients: ripe fruit, fresh dairy products, and the best-quality chocolate available to you. A great pie also needs a well-executed crust: flaky, flavorful, and cooked through. By following a few key principles about ingredient temperature, mixing, handling, relaxing, and baking, you'll find the perfect piecrust is easily attainable.

The liquids and fats should be well chilled before they are incorporated into the dough. Chilled fat keeps the gluten in the flour from becoming tough. Work the fat completely into the flour before adding the final liquid. Manipulate the dough delicately, without pulling at it or tugging it. The dough will shrink and become tough or distorted with unnecessary handling. Handle the dough quickly, lightly, and with confidence. Rest the dough before baking. Give the gluten a short time to relax; the dough will shrink less when heat is introduced. The oven should always be hot before the constructed pie is baked. Understand the recipe completely before you begin, so you can work as quickly and efficiently as possible at every step.

Unless collecting kitchen gadgets is your hobby, keep your pie equipment simple. You will need a sturdy rolling pin. The most durable ones are usually made of hardwood and come with or without handles. Dough can be made by hand, with a knife or a pastry blade, or by machine, either a handheld mixer or a freestanding machine. I am partial to a freestanding mixer, mainly because I make a lot of dough. For the best results, I incorporate all the ingredients with a paddle attachment, then gather the dough together by hand and roll it out immediately. The dough then rests in the refrigerator already in the pie or tart plate. It sets up firm and is ready to bake almost as soon as the filling goes in.

Pie plates generally come in 8-inch, 9-inch, 9½-inch, and 10-inch sizes. The shallowest plates are about an inch deep; the deepest are about 2½ to 3 inches deep. Pie plates are made of various materials, from stainless steel to Pyrex, glass, and ceramic. Pies baked in thick ceramic and Pyrex will take a bit more time to bake than pies baked in metal pans.

For fruit pies, I prefer a deep dish that will hold in the juices and the fruit. A tart requires a straight-sided, shallow tart pan that produces a thin, elegant tart. Tart pans come in various sizes and styles. They are distinguished by their short (½ inch to 1 inch), straight sides, as opposed to the sloping sides of pie plates. Most useful are tart pans with removable bottoms that allow you to gently raise your tart out of its mold and serve it either directly from the insert or after sliding it onto a plate.

Tinfoil and waxed paper are basic supplies that will be needed. They are handy for blind baking—cooking a pie shell without the filling—and for transferring raw dough from table to pie plate. So be sure to have these supplies at hand for when you need them. A few inexpensive tools are all you need to begin.

When a pie shell needs to be baked before being filled with a filling, you must "blind bake" your pie. To keep the sides of your pie or tart from collapsing, it becomes necessary to line the pie with a piece of paper or foil and fill that covering with weights. Special ceramic and metal pellets, referred to as pie weights, are available for this purpose. More affordably, uncooked rice, split peas, or any other kind of dry bean will work just as well. Fill your pie with the chosen weight and bake for 15 minutes. Remove the weights and paper when the crust appears dry and has begun to brown. Add your filling, and continue to bake until the pie is fully cooked.

PERFECT PIE DOUGH

This recipe makes a perfect two-crust pie every time. With a little bit of butter and a little bit of short-ening, the recipe achieves the perfect balance between taste and texture. Piecrust can also be made by using only butter or only shortening, or by substituting extra of one for the other. Just make certain the total amount of fat is the same as indicated in the original recipe. Butter gives the crust a more delicious flavor, while shortening makes a flakier crust.

Lard can be used in place of butter for all or part of the total fat content and will result in the flakiest, most flavorful pies possible.

If your diet doesn't include lard, butter, or any extra cholesterol, use shortening while making a piecrust. Additionally, eggs and butter in a filling can be replaced with a few tablespoons of tapioca, flour, or cornstarch.

2½ cups flour
1 teaspoon salt
3 tablespoons sugar
¾ cup or 1½ sticks butter
¼ cup shortening
5–6 tablespoons ice-cold water

In a mixing bowl, combine the flour, salt, and sugar. Cut the butter into small cubes. Make sure to keep the butter as cold as possible at all times. Add the fats (the butter and the shortening) into the mixing bowl, and cut the fat into the flour using a knife or the paddle attachment of a mixer. When the flour resembles coarse sand, add the cold water. Use the water sparingly, and stop adding the water when the dough begins to come together. Turn off the mixer, and finish bringing the dough to-gether into a firm ball by hand. Mix the dough as little as possible to keep it tender.

Separate the dough into two equal-sized balls, and press them into flat disks. Lightly flour a counter surface, and flour the dough lightly. Roll the dough into round disks ⅛ inch thick. To keep the dough round, turn the dough 1 inch clockwise after every roll of the rolling pin. Continue to flour the counter as you roll your dough to keep it from sticking: support the dough on the rolling pin, and spread fresh flour in the area where the dough will be rolled. When the dough is roughly ⅛ inch thick and can easily cover the pie tin with 1-inch overhang, it is ready for use. Roll the dough loosely onto the rolling pin, and transfer it to the pie tin. The dough can also be transported by wax paper and lowered into the pie tin from the support of the paper. Gently work the dough into the bottom and sides of the pie tin, being careful not to tug or pull on the dough. When the dough sits snugly in the tin, chill the dough for at least half an hour in the refrigerator. Often, recipes call for resting the dough in the refrigerator before rolling. This makes the dough more difficult to roll and causes it to crack because of its firmness. It is much more efficient to roll the dough out before resting.

HEIRLOOM PIE DOUGH

If you want to make dough days in advance and hold it in the refrigerator, make an heirloom pastry. Add 1 tablespoon of vinegar in place of 1 tablespoon of the water, and this dough will keep well in the refrigerator for weeks.

TIPS FOR GUARANTEED SUCCESS

Keep the fats (butter, shortening, or lard) as cold as possible for the flakiest crust.
Roll your dough as soon as it is mixed.
Rest your dough in the pie plate in the refrigerator for half an hour.
Don't pull and tug at your dough.
If you prebake a pie shell, bake it until it is done to avoid soggy crusts.

CREAM CHEESE PIE DOUGH

Makes 1
double-crust pie

This dough is particularly good with tart cherry pie and mixed-berry turnovers. The recipe should make one pie with a lattice crust or one recipe of little fried pies.

2 cups flour
1 teaspoon salt
2 tablespoons sugar
½ cup butter
8 ounces cream cheese

Combine the flour, sugar, and salt. Cut up the butter and the cream cheese into pea-sized pieces. Incorporate the butter first. When the flour resembles coarse sand, add the cream cheese and mix until combined. Finish the dough by working it into a flat disk by hand. Roll immediately to ⅛ inch thick and work into pie plate, or leave flat to cut out fried pies or turnovers.

CHEDDAR CHEESE CRUST

This crust is particularly good with apple pie or a savory pie. Just add cheddar cheese in place of cream cheese, and bring the dough together with a few tablespoons of cold water.

i ♥ pies and tarts

COOKIE CRUST

In a pinch this crust does not need to be baked. Just press the crumbs into the pie tin, and it's ready.

1½ cups graham cracker, vanilla wafer, chocolate wafer, or macaroon crumbs
3 tablespoons sugar
½ teaspoon salt
⅓ cup butter, melted

Preheat the oven to 350°F. Toss together cookie crumbs, sugar, and salt. Pour melted butter over crumbs and work the mixture by hand until all the crumbs are coated with butter. Press the crumbs into a 9-inch pie tin that has been lightly greased.

Bake the crumbs for 5 to 10 minutes. Remove the crust from the oven, and allow to cool completely before adding any filling.

SWEET TART DOUGH

In contrast to the flaky tenderness of pie dough, the sweet tart dough has the taste and texture of a sugar cookie. This recipe will make enough dough for the bottom of one tart. Different rules of handling apply to tart dough. Tart dough is much more fragile than pie dough, but much more forgiving. If it breaks or rips, just press it back together, and there will be no evidence of the tear.

1¼ cups flour
1 teaspoon salt
½ cup confectioners' sugar
½ cup butter
1 egg yolk
1 teaspoon vanilla

Combine the flour, salt, and sugar in a mixing bowl. Cut the chilled butter into small cubes and add to the flour mixture. Using a knife or the paddle attachment of a mixer, incorporate the butter into the flour mixture until it resembles coarse sand. Add in the egg yolk and vanilla; mix until combined. The dough will appear dry and powdery in the bowl. Keep working the mixture by hand until it comes together in a ball. The dough should hold together when you squeeze it in your hand. Do not add more liquid until you have tried to work the dough into a ball by hand.

VARIATIONS

To make chocolate dough, add ¼ cup of cocoa powder to the recipe. To make almond dough, add ¼ cup of ground almonds to the dough. To make cornmeal dough, add ½ cup of cornmeal to the recipe. If you are making a dough variation, add 1 or 2 teaspoons of water to help bring the dough together.

NO-ROLL PIE DOUGH

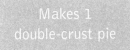

Makes 1
double-crust pie

My mother gave me this recipe for pie dough that never needs to be rolled. She used to hand it out in a foods-for-entertaining class she taught in the 1960s, that odd time in culinary history when home cooks became convinced that cooking at home was difficult, instead of a natural occurrence.

2¼ cups flour
2 tablespoons sugar
2 teaspoons salt
¾ cup oil
3 tablespoons milk

Sift the dry ingredients into the pie tin. Add the oil and milk to the pie tin and mix until the flour is moistened. Press the dough evenly, firmly, and quickly into the bottom edges of the pie tin. Fill or weight as needed. Bake at 425°F for 12 to 15 minutes.

SAVORY TART DOUGH

This strong dough is not at all sweet and can stand up to the rigors of a tart with a liquid filling.

2 cups flour
1 teaspoon salt
1 tablespoon sugar
7 tablespoons butter
6 tablespoons water
1 egg

Combine the flour, salt, and sugar with the butter, and mix until the butter is completely incorporated with the flour. Whisk the egg with the water, and add to the flour mixture. Knead the dough by hand to bring it completely together.

Roll the dough immediately and place in desired tart pan. This dough is usually prebaked, supported by pie weights.

The bottom crust of your pie should always hang about an inch over the pie plate. This allows you to tuck the dough under itself and into the pie plate. The resulting lip can be crimped with a fork or your fingers. Any top dough should be tucked under this lip before crimping to seal the pie shut.

How you finish the top of your pie is largely up to you. Whether you simply cover it with a top piece of dough, slash it for ventilation, or create an elaborate lattice is a matter of preference.

For a juicy fruit pie, like rhubarb or sour cherry, it is best to create a top with a lot of ventilation to allow the steam of cooking fruit to escape. An open lattice is nice for this kind of pie, or a top crust with large 1- to 2-inch cutouts made with a round or heart-shaped cookie cutter. Cutting out tiny leaf or flower shapes with mini cookie cutters and applying them with water to the rim of the pie or on top of a plain top crust creates a festive holiday border or a fancy party dessert. The effect is dramatic and appears complicated, but is actually quite simple.

I wish I could say I thought of this next technique myself, but I first saw it at a country fair. Simplicity is genius, particularly in a craft such as pie making. Grate pie dough over your filling using a large grater, the one usually reserved for grating cheese. Make an even layer of pie dough over the top and bake as directed. I like to add slivered almonds and sugar along with the grated dough for a crunchy, nutty finish.

The top dough can be brushed with milk, cream, or a wash made with egg and a little water. This will give the piecrust a deep, rich color. Granulated sugar can be sprinkled on top before cooking, or confectioners' sugar can be sprinkled on after. Obviously, pies that will not be baked after they are filled and tarts do not need a top crust. These pies and tarts can be finished with flavored whipped creams, candy, candied fruit, fresh fruit, or chocolate curls.

notes

all-american fruit pies

FARM STAND APPLE PIE	15
TRUE BLUEBERRY PIE	17
DEEP-DISH SOUR CHERRY PIE	19
PRIZE-WINNING PEACH PIE	20
RHUBARB STRAWBERRY PIE	22
RASPBERRY CUSTARD PIE	24
PEAR RAISIN OATMEAL CRISP	26
APPLE CRANBERRY BROWN BETTY	27
FROZEN STRAWBERRY CLOUD PIE	29

These pies started the great tradition of pie making. Local fruits baked between two layers of dough offered symbols of hospitality and abundance—pies like apple, peach, and sour cherry; desserts that you can find at farmer's markets and roadside stands across the country.

Fresh fruits are tossed with a little thickener—cornstarch, flour, or tapioca—and sugar, maybe a little lemon juice or salt, and baked between flaky crusts. The preparation is simple, the finished product convenient and tasty. These recipes are a starting point, formulas open to experimentation and personal variation.

FARM STAND APPLE PIE

This pie is a big double-crusted American classic. Piles of tart apples are cooked between layers of flaky dough, producing the perfect combination of tart and sweet with a whisper of cinnamon.

7 Granny Smith apples or other tart baking apple (peeled, cored, and sliced into ½-inch wedges)
½ lemon, juiced, or 2 tablespoons lemon juice
2 tablespoons flour
½ cup sugar
1 teaspoon cinnamon
½ teaspoon salt
3 tablespoons butter
1 recipe prepared Perfect Pie Dough (p. 4), rolled and chilled for half an hour in a 10-inch pie plate

PREHEAT THE OVEN TO 375°F.

Place the prepared apples in a large bowl, and sprinkle with lemon juice. Toss the apples to cover them evenly with the juice. In a separate bowl, combine flour, sugar, cinnamon, and salt. Toss the combined dry ingredients with the apples.

Pile the apples into the prepared pie plate, creating an even mound. Dot the apples with the butter. Lifting the second piece of dough on your rolling pin, evenly cover the apples and the butter. Tuck the edges of both the bottom and the top pieces of dough under and into the pie plate. Working all the way around the pie plate, crimp the edge with a fork to seal the dough. Cut slits in the dough to allow the steam to escape from the pie as it cooks.

Bake the pie for 60 to 70 minutes. After 45 minutes, turn down the oven to prevent the dough from becoming too dark. Continue baking the pie at 325°F for the remaining 15 to 25 minutes. Bake the pie until the crust is golden brown and the filling is bubbling. The pie is done when a knife can easily be inserted into the pie and removed without resistance.

Apple pie is delicious served with lightly sweetened whipped cream, vanilla or cinnamon ice cream, or a glass of cold milk. For a change, serve your pie with a wedge of aged cheddar. The salty, caramel taste of an older cheddar goes perfectly with apple pie in this old-fashioned Pennsylvania pairing.

TRUE BLUEBERRY PIE

Blueberries have gotten a lot of good press because of their reputation as a "brain food." They are high in vitamins, contain healthful antioxidants, and make a delicious pie filling. Blueberries are available most of the year, but are usually best in the summer months. Quick-frozen blueberries are an easy substitution and usually have the best blueberry flavor during the cold months. Use the blueberries frozen, right out of the bag, for best results.

5 cups blueberries (remove stems and green berries)
2 tablespoons lemon juice
1 cup sugar
4 tablespoons quick-cooking tapioca
1 tablespoon lemon zest
1 tablespoon orange zest
½ teaspoon salt
3 tablespoons butter
1 recipe prepared Cream Cheese Pie Dough (p. 6) or Perfect Pie Dough (p. 4), rolled and chilled for half
    an hour in a 10-inch pie plate

PREHEAT THE OVEN TO 350°F.

Place the blueberries in a large bowl, and sprinkle them with the lemon juice. In a separate, smaller bowl, combine the sugar, tapioca, salt, and lemon and orange zests. Toss the dry ingredients with the blueberries, and allow the mixture to sit while you prepare the pie plate.

Using a small cookie cutter (about 1 inch across), cut three holes for the steam to escape in the top crust.

Pile the blueberries into the pie shell, and dot the butter over the top of the blueberries. Cover them with the top crust. Tucking the edge of the top shell under the bottom dough, firmly seal the pie around the edge. Crimp the edge with the back of a fork.

Bake the pie at 350°F for 40 to 50 minutes. The pie is done when the crust is deep brown and the filling is dark and thickened.

VARIATION

Blueberry pie filling can also be made quickly on the stove top. Allow 2½ cups of blueberries to simmer with the tapioca, lemon juice, sugar, salt, and zests until it thickens. Remove the blueberries from the heat, and stir in the butter and the remaining 2½ cups blueberries; allow the filling to cool. The filling can then be placed in a pie tin with a Cookie Crust (p. 7) or Perfect Pie Dough (p. 4) that has already been cooked. Garnish the top with fresh whipped cream.

DEEP-DISH SOUR CHERRY PIE

Makes one 10-inch deep-dish pie

The season for fresh sour cherries is very short, but the extraordinary flavor of these cherries is worth looking for. A cherry or olive pitter will make the job of removing the stones easier. Sour cherries are most easily found canned or jarred, and canned cherries have the added benefit of already having the pits removed.

6 cups sour cherries (cleaned and stones removed) or 2 cans sour cherries
1⅓ cups sugar
¼ cup instant tapioca (3 tablespoons for canned cherries)
¼ teaspoon salt
4 tablespoons butter
3 tablespoons milk (for crust)
1 recipe prepared Cream Cheese Pie Dough (p. 6) or Perfect Pie Dough (p. 4), rolled and chilled for half
    an hour in pie plate

PREHEAT THE OVEN TO 375°F.

In a medium bowl, combine the cherries with the sugar and tapioca. (If you are using canned cherries, drain them and retain ½ cup of liquid for the pie. Add the sugar and the tapioca to the liquid.) Let the fruit mixture sit for 15 minutes to allow the tapioca to hydrate.

Remove the rested and prepared pie dough from the refrigerator, and fill the pie with the cherry filling. Cover the pie with a decorative top, and brush with milk and granulated sugar to garnish.

Bake at 375°F for 50 to 60 minutes. When the crust is golden brown and filling slowly bubbles, the pie is done.

A NOTE ABOUT CHERRIES

Sweet cherries, red bing cherries, or white Rainier cherries can be made into a pie as well, but their flavor is quite different from that of the sour cherry. When making a sweet cherry pie, add 2 tablespoons of lime juice, 2 teaspoons of lime zest, and 2 teaspoons of vanilla. Prepare it with a crunchy topping for added flavor, for example, Almond Coconut Crumble (p. 28).

PRIZE-WINNING PEACH PIE

This rich, delicious pie is best when peaches are in season in the late summer. Look for peaches that are ripe but not overly ripe. Nectarines, plums, or other stone fruits can be substituted for the peaches.

8 medium peaches (peeled, stones removed, and sliced into ½-inch wedges), about 5 cups
1 lemon, juiced
4 tablespoons flour
⅔ cup sugar
1 teaspoon salt
½ cup butter, melted
4 egg yolks
1 recipe prepared Perfect Pie Dough (p. 4), rolled and chilled for half an hour in a 9½- to 10-inch pie plate

PREHEAT THE OVEN TO 350°F.

Place the prepared peaches in a large bowl. Toss the peaches with the lemon juice. In a separate bowl, combine the flour, sugar, and salt. Toss the dry ingredients with the peaches. Add the butter and egg yolks, and mix thoroughly.

Heap the peach filling into the prepared pie shell.

Using your favorite 2-inch cookie cutter—a star shape or maybe a heart—cut out five shapes in the dough for the top. Not only does this provide the needed means of escape for the steam, it creates an attractive decoration for your pie. Tuck the ends of the top dough under the bottom crust, and crimp the dough all around with your fingers.

Bake the pie for 45 to 60 minutes, until the juices begin to boil in large, slow bubbles. The pie is finished when the crust is deep brown and a knife can easily be inserted into the pie and removed without resistance.

ALTERNATE FINISHING TOUCHES

I like to make a lattice with plenty of open holes to top a fresh fruit pie such as cherry, peach, or rhubarb. The open spaces allow the steam to escape easily from the cooking fruit. The crust is drier and the filling firmer.

To create an attractive lattice, first roll your top piece of dough to ⅛ inch thick. Allow the dough to rest on a separate plate while the bottom of the pie rests in the pie plate. When the time comes to finish the pie, cut even strips from the firm top dough. The strips should be about ½ inch wide and can be cut freehand or with a ruler to keep them straight. To make the job even easier, use a pizza cutter or fluted ravioli wheel to make the strips.

The next part can be a little tricky. Lay one set of strips side by side across the pie. Weave the remaining strips into the first set, making a basket pattern in and out of the first set of strips on the pie. When you have completely covered your pie, trim the ends of the strips and tuck them under the lip of the bottom crust. Crimp the edges to seal the pie.

RHUBARB STRAWBERRY PIE

Rhubarb grows in the early spring in many parts of the United States, making it one of the first pie fruits (though technically a vegetable) to arrive with the warm weather. Rhubarb will continue to grow all summer long. If your rhubarb is particularly old, peel the strings off the outside of the ribs with a knife or a vegetable peeler. The pie will be less stringy.

4 cups rhubarb, cleaned and cut into 1-inch sticks
3 cups strawberries, cleaned and sliced
½ cup quick-cooking tapioca
2 cups sugar
2 teaspoons orange zest
½ teaspoon salt
1 recipe prepared Perfect Pie Dough (p. 4), rolled and chilled for half an hour in a pie plate

PREHEAT THE OVEN TO 350°F.

Combine the rhubarb and strawberries in a large bowl and toss with the sugar, tapioca, orange zest, and salt. Allow this fruit mixture to sit at room temperature for 15 minutes, so the tapioca can hydrate.

Using a ruler and a knife, cut ½-inch strips out of the piece of dough you have set aside for the top of the pie. Remove the prepared pie shell from the refrigerator and fill with pie filling. Using the strips of dough, create a basket weave or lattice on top of the pie. Brush the lattice with whole milk, and sprinkle with additional sugar. Tuck the ends of the strips of dough under the overlap from the bottom crust, and crimp the edges to seal the dough.

Bake for 50 to 60 minutes until the crust is golden brown and the filling bubbles slowly in nickel-sized bubbles. Allow the pie to set for 1 hour before serving.

i ♥ pies and tarts

The uninitiated sometimes find the acidic and sour taste of rhubarb too harsh; as a result, rhubarb is usually combined with fresh strawberries. These summer garden neighbors complement each other by enhancing the flavor and texture of one another.

RHUBARB-LOVER'S PIE

If you are familiar with the unique taste of rhubarb and would prefer to make a pie using only rhubarb, use 6 to 7 cups of rhubarb and increase the sugar to 2½ cups. Otherwise, follow the above recipe.

If you wish to make a pie using only strawberries, try the Fresh Berry Tart (p. 99). The delicate flavor of strawberries is best when they are uncooked and enriched with just a little pastry cream and a cornmeal crust.

RASPBERRY CUSTARD PIE

Raspberry Custard Pie is delicious in mid- to late summer, when the raspberries are in season. Juicy and overripe, they make a great pie, particularly when they are combined with rich buttermilk custard. The raspberries create a starburst of color on the custard that is beautiful as well as delicious.

2 pints ripe raspberries
5 tablespoons flour
1½ cups sugar
⅔ cup buttermilk
½ cup butter, melted
3 eggs
1 teaspoon vanilla
1 tablespoon orange zest
1 recipe prepared Perfect Pie Dough (p. 4), rolled and chilled for half an hour in a 9- to 10-inch pie
    plate

PREHEAT THE OVEN TO 425°F.

Toss the raspberries in a bowl with 2 tablespoons of flour and ¼ cup of sugar and set aside.

Line the prepared pie shell with greased tinfoil, and fill with dried beans or pie weights. Place the pie shell in the oven, and bake for 20 minutes. Turn the oven down to 350°F, and remove the tinfoil and weights from the pie. Continue baking until the pie shell no longer appears wet and has begun to turn a light golden color.

While the pie shell is baking, warm the buttermilk and melted butter in a saucepan. Break the eggs into a small bowl, and whisk in the remaining flour and sugar, vanilla, and orange zest. When the buttermilk begins to simmer, temper it into the egg mixture by whisking it in ¼ cup at a time. Return the mixture to the stove, and cook for several minutes over medium heat.

When the pie shell is golden, add the raspberries to the shell and fill with the buttermilk custard. Return the pie to the 350°F oven for 30 to 40 minutes. Bake until filling is set and jiggles only slightly when shaken.

QUICK BUTTERMILK
If you don't have easy access to buttermilk, combine ⅔ cup of regular milk with 1 tablespoon of vinegar or lemon juice to sour it.

PEAR RAISIN OATMEAL CRISP

Crisps can be made with or without bottom crusts. Pear Raisin Oatmeal Crisp is made with a bottom crust that adds a little more richness to the pear filling.

6 large, ripe pears (peeled, cored, and diced into ½-inch pieces)
2 tart apples (peeled, cored, and diced into ½-inch pieces)
1 tablespoon lemon juice
¼ cup flour
½ cup sugar
½ cup golden raisins
1 teaspoon cinnamon
½ recipe prepared Perfect Pie Dough (p. 4), rolled and chilled for half an hour in a 10-inch pie plate
1 recipe Oatmeal Crisp Topping (see below)

PREHEAT THE OVEN TO 350°F.

In a large bowl, toss together the pears and apples. Sprinkle the fruit with lemon juice. In a separate small bowl, mix the flour, sugar, and cinnamon. Add the dry ingredients to the fruit and combine thoroughly. Stir in the raisins.

Fill the pie plate with the fruit mixture and top with the oatmeal topping.

Bake at 350°F for 60 to 70 minutes. The crisp is finished when the topping is a deep brown and the filling bubbles slowly.

oatmeal crisp topping

For a delicious and filling oatmeal crisp topping, combine ½ cup of flour, 1 cup of oatmeal, ½ teaspoon of cinnamon, ¼ teaspoon of salt, and 6 tablespoons of softened butter. Mix all of the ingredients with a fork until the topping forms large clumps. Sprinkle on top of the filling.

APPLE CRANBERRY BROWN BETTY

Makes one
2-quart casserole

A brown Betty is a homey, old-fashioned dessert that is quick and easy to make. It scoops easily out of a casserole dish and is delicious with a side of cinnamon whipped cream.

one 14.4-ounce box graham crackers
1 teaspoon cinnamon
½ teaspoon nutmeg
¾ cup (1½ sticks) butter, melted
5 tart apples (peeled, cored, and diced into ½-inch pieces)
3 tablespoons lemon juice
2 tablespoons flour
¼ cup sugar
1 cup fresh or frozen cranberries

PREHEAT THE OVEN TO 350°F.

Crush the graham crackers in their sleeves, and then empty them one sleeve at a time into a bowl or, preferably, a food processor. Pulse the crackers to make fine crumbs, or crush the graham crackers in a bowl, if you do not have a food processor. To the crumbs add the cinnamon and nutmeg. Toss the crumbs with the melted butter, and incorporate the butter well.

In a separate bowl, combine the apples, lemon juice, flour, sugar, and cranberries. Cover the bottom of a square 2-quart casserole dish with the graham cracker crumb mixture; press down firmly to create a bottom crust. Cover the crust with half of the apples. Place another layer of crumbs over the apples, and then add another layer of apples. Save enough crumbs to cover the top of the brown Betty with crumbs.

Bake for 40 minutes at 350°F. Test the filling with a knife; when the apples are tender, the brown Betty is finished.

ALMOND COCONUT CRUMBLE

A pie or crumble topping can be a combination of any cracker, cookie, nut, sweet bread crouton, coconut, or spice, bound together by a little butter or margarine and sweetened with sugar. One of my favorites is Almond Coconut Crumble: Cream ½ cup of butter with ½ cup brown sugar and 1 teaspoon of salt; add 1 cup of flour into the mixture when you are done. Fold in 1 cup of almonds, ½ cup coconut flakes, and 1 teaspoon vanilla. Generously sprinkle over pie filling and bake.

FROZEN STRAWBERRY CLOUD PIE

Strawberry Cloud Pie stands dramatically tall, a frozen whipped dessert that tastes like a cloud of frozen strawberries. It is delicious in the summertime straight from the freezer with whipped cream and ripe berries.

one 10-ounce package of frozen strawberries
2 egg whites
⅛ teaspoon salt
⅔ cup sugar
1 tablespoon lemon juice
1 tablespoon vanilla
1 cup heavy cream, whipped
additional fresh strawberries for garnish
1 recipe prepared vanilla, chocolate, or graham cracker Cookie Crust (p. 7)

Place egg whites, salt, sugar, lemon juice, vanilla, and partially thawed strawberries in a mixing bowl. Whisk on medium speed until the mixture becomes light and fluffy. Fold in 1 cup of whipped heavy cream or 1 cup whipped nondairy topping.

Shovel the mixture in big spoonfuls into the prepared cookie crust. Freeze the pie until you are ready to serve it.

Serve with additional whipped cream and fresh berries.

Note: The consumption of raw egg whites is not recommended for everybody.

BERRY GARNISH

Fresh berries make a beautiful garnish for many pies. Simply adding a strawberry cut in half or in quarters makes a dessert look better. Cutting a strawberry in half and then cutting the halves into fans makes a dessert look elegant. Berries of contrasting colors, like blueberries or blackberries, bring out the color of the pie.

traditional favorites

BOURBON PECAN PIE	33
TOASTED COCONUT CUSTARD PIE	35
CARAMELIZED BANANA CREAM PIE	36
KEY LIME PIE	38
MILE-HIGH LEMON MERINGUE PIE	39
PINEAPPLE CHESS PIE	41
PUMPKIN CHEESECAKE PIE	43
SOUTHERN SWEET POTATO PIE	45
LIME DAIQUIRI CHIFFON PIE	47
AMISH VANILLA PIE	49
SOUR CREAM RAISIN PIE	50

I can still remember the first time my parents took me out for dinner. We went to the local diner, a bustling, shiny, steel-sided building filled with waitresses in too-tight uniforms and tables decorated with dusty plastic flowers. Being dragged by the hand through the door, I remember looking up in awe at the towering display of glass-enclosed pies. Lemon meringue pie stood impossibly tall, peaks of meringue lightly browned. Coconut custard, banana cream, cheesecake, and clouds of citrus chiffon, all lined up in rows. Their uncut sides faced forward, ready to seduce any customer if the waitresses' charms failed. These are the traditional favorites: the diner classics, the homemade holiday staples, and the time-tested family favorites.

BOURBON PECAN PIE

Makes one
9½-inch pie

Bourbon Pecan Pie is one of my favorite Thanksgiving pies. Loaded with chocolate chips and dried tart cherries soaked in bourbon, it tastes better every day that it sits. Try to find good-quality Michigan dried tart cherries for the best flavor.

½ cup dried tart cherries
6 tablespoons bourbon
4 eggs
¾ cup brown sugar
1 teaspoon salt
¼ cup molasses
¼ cup corn syrup
4 tablespoons butter, melted
½ cup chocolate chips
3 cups pecan halves
1 recipe prepared Sweet Tart Dough (p. 8), rolled into a tart pan and chilled for half an hour

A few hours before you are ready to make your pie, cover the dried cherries with simmering water. When they begin to soften, after about half an hour, drain off the water, and pour bourbon over the tart cherries. Let them soak until needed in the recipe.

PREHEAT THE OVEN TO 350°F.

Whisk the eggs in a medium bowl with the brown sugar, salt, molasses, and corn syrup. To this mixture add the butter. Fold in the chocolate chips, bourbon, tart cherries, and pecans. Pour the mixture into the unbaked, prepared tart shell. Be careful to keep the filling well within the dough. Bake for 40 minutes at 350°F. The pie is finished when the filling is firm and the crust is brown.

Any spills or leakage will become like glue when you try to remove the tart from the pan. If your pie filling does leak and become stuck to the pan, allow it to cool completely. Then heat it for 5 minutes in a very hot oven, and work the tart out of the pan with a knife.

USING DRIED FRUITS

Raisins, currants, prunes, and dried cherries, blueberries, and cranberries are all readily available most times of the year. These dried fruits are most enjoyable in baked goods when they have been hydrated in a little simmering water. This makes them a little softer and juicier. Soak your favorite dried fruit in a little alcohol overnight for some added flavor. I like to soak my tart cherries in bourbon or my prunes in Armagnac (a French brandy). If you are using dried pears, try soaking them in pear liqueur. Be careful how much hard alcohol you add to the recipe, as it is quite strong.

TOASTED COCONUT CUSTARD PIE

Makes one
9½-inch pie

This true American classic has been improved by the addition of more coconut flavor from canned coconut milk. A coconut-and-rum caramel sauce is an added attraction to a time-tested favorite.

⅔ cup milk

⅔ cup unsweetened coconut milk

½ teaspoon salt

4 large eggs

1 cup sugar

3 tablespoons flour

2 tablespoons rum

1 recipe prepared vanilla or chocolate Cookie Crust (p. 7), baked and cooled

2 cups sweetened, shredded coconut, toasted

½ cup chocolate chips (optional)

1 recipe Coconut-and-Rum Caramel Sauce (see below)

In a medium saucepan, combine the milk with the coconut milk and salt, and bring the liquid to a simmer. Break 4 eggs into a medium bowl. Combine the flour and sugar, and whisk them with the eggs. Slowly add the hot milk to the egg mixture, ¼ cup at a time. Return the mixture to the saucepan, and bring to a simmer, stirring constantly. The mixture will thicken into a pastry cream. Remove the pan from the heat, and whisk in the rum. Stir in 1 cup of the toasted coconut. Pour the mixture immediately into the pie shell, and cover the top with the remaining toasted coconut and (if desired) chocolate chips.

coconut-and-rum caramel sauce

Use the coconut milk left over from the pie to make a delicious sauce. Combine the coconut milk, ¾ cup of milk, and 2 tablespoons of sugar. Simmer the mixture slowly over a low flame for 30 to 40 minutes, until the liquid is a thick golden brown. Remove the caramel that has been created, and thin it with a few drops of rum. Place the pie on a serving plate, and drizzle it with the Coconut-and-Rum Caramel Sauce.

CARAMELIZED BANANA CREAM PIE

Makes one
10-inch pie

Pudding and bananas are layered under a meringue top to create Caramelized Banana Cream Pie. The bananas are cooked to enhance their sweet flavor and discourage discoloration.

4 ripe bananas, sliced into oblong coins ⅛ inch thick
5 tablespoons butter
2 tablespoons lemon juice
1 cup sugar
¼ cup cornstarch
2 cups milk
2 eggs
1 teaspoon vanilla
½ teaspoon salt
1 recipe prepared vanilla Cookie Crust (p. 7), baked and cooled
1 recipe Meringue Topping (from Mile-High Lemon Meringue Pie, p. 40)

In a large sauté pan, melt 2 tablespoons of butter. Warm the butter until it bubbles. Sprinkle ⅓ cup of sugar into the pan, and then add the bananas. Sear the bananas on both sides at medium-high heat, and allow them to caramelize and cook completely. Remove the bananas from the saucepan, and sprinkle the pan with the lemon juice. Shake the pan to loosen any caramelized fruit from the pan. Allow the bananas to cool on a separate plate.

In a medium saucepan, warm the milk with another ⅓ cup of sugar and ½ teaspoon of salt. Allow the remaining 3 tablespoons of butter to melt in the warming milk. Bring the milk to a gentle simmer.

Combine the remaining ⅓ cup of sugar with the cornstarch in a small bowl. Break the 2 eggs into a medium bowl, and using a whisk, incorporate the sugar and cornstarch into the eggs.

When the eggs, sugar, and cornstarch are completely mixed, begin tempering the milk into the egg mixture by slowly add the milk, ¼ cup at a time. After the milk has been completely combined with the eggs, return the mixture to the saucepan and whisk the milk mixture over medium heat until it slowly simmers and thickens. Be careful to keep scraping out the corners of the pot, so the filling doesn't burn and ruin the flavor.

Layer the pastry cream and the bananas into the pie shell while they are still warm. Cover the pie with plastic wrap to keep a skin from forming.

PREHEAT THE OVEN TO 450°F.

Immediately prepare the meringue, and top the pie with a piped meringue while the pudding is still warm. Caramelize the top of the meringue by browning it for 8 minutes in a 450°F oven.

SHORTCUT

Vanilla or banana pudding from a box can be used instead of making a filling from scratch. For added banana flavor, incorporate a caramelized banana into the pudding by mixing it with a blender or food processor.

KEY LIME PIE

Key Lime Pie is a new American classic. The unique sweet, acidic taste of tiny key limes complements any meal with a tropical finish.

4 ounces cream cheese
4 egg yolks
one 14-ounce can sweetened condensed milk
¾ cup key lime juice
2 teaspoons lime zest (if using fresh key limes)
½ teaspoon salt
1 recipe prepared graham cracker Cookie Crust (p. 7)

PREHEAT THE OVEN TO 350°F.

Using a hand mixer or paddle attachment, incorporate the egg yolks one at a time into the cream cheese. When the egg yolks have been completely combined, add the condensed milk slowly. Into this mixture add the lime juice, zest, and salt. Pour the completed filling into a prepared graham cracker crust, and bake at 350°F for 30 minutes. When the custard sets (wobbles only slightly when shaken), remove the pie from the oven. Allow the pie to cool, and refrigerate it when it reaches room temperature.

MORE ABOUT KEY LIME JUICE

Key lime juice is available by the bottle in a lot of grocery stores and many gourmet food stores. If your local stores don't carry it, it is easily obtained on the Internet. The season for fresh key limes is short, mainly during the summer months. If you can get the limes fresh, they require a little bit of effort to juice because they are tiny, but the result is well worth the effort.

MILE-HIGH LEMON MERINGUE PIE

Makes 1 tall
10-inch pie

The dramatic spikes of fresh Mile-High Lemon Meringue Pie herald the delicious lemony center that lies inside. Make and eat a lemon meringue pie on the same day. Not only does the quality of the meringue suffer as it sits, the lightly cooked meringue should not be allowed to wait.

4 eggs, separated
1⅓ cups sugar
⅓ cup cornstarch
¾ cup lemon juice
¾ cup water
3 tablespoons butter, melted
zest of one lemon
1 recipe prepared graham cracker Cookie Crust (p. 7), baked and cooled
1 recipe prepared Meringue Topping (p. 40)

PREHEAT THE OVEN TO 350°F.

Place the four yolks in a medium bowl. Whisk ⅓ cup of sugar and the cornstarch into the yolks. Slowly whisk in the lemon juice and water. Add the remainder of the sugar. Stir until sugar dissolves.

Transfer the mixture to a small saucepan, and bring it to a simmer over medium heat. Simmer for about 5 minutes, and remove the lemon custard from the heat. Whisk in butter and lemon zest. Pour the filling immediately into a completely cooled pie shell, and cover with plastic wrap.

Begin to prepare the meringue immediately, and when it is ready, remove the plastic wrap and cover the pie with meringue. Be sure to apply the meringue while the filling is hot, and be sure the meringue touches the pie shell everywhere to help stabilize it. After heaping on all the meringue, use the back of a spoon to create a spiked effect by touching the meringue and then pulling back the spoon, raising the meringue into the air in peaks.

Place the pie in a preheated 350°F oven, and bake until the spikes are brown, about 10 to 12 minutes. Watch pie carefully to make sure it doesn't burn.

meringue topping

To make a meringue topping for the pie, begin with a clean, dry bowl, preferably the bowl of a stand mixer. Add to the bowl the 4 egg whites (which remain from the lemon filling). Using a whisk, slowly begin to mix the egg whites with ½ teaspoon of cream of tartar and 1 cup of sugar. Warm the egg whites gently over a pot of simmering water until they are quite warm to the touch. Whisk continually to prevent the egg whites from cooking to the bowl. When the eggs are frothy and quite warm, attach the bowl to a mixer with a whisk attachment. Whisk until cool. When the eggs are glossy and form soft peaks, add ½ teaspoon of vanilla. Whisk until the meringue forms stiff peaks. Use the meringue immediately. I prefer to use this style of meringue, called Swiss meringue, because the egg whites get a chance to cook and the resulting meringue is more stable and less likely to weep.

PINEAPPLE CHESS PIE

Pineapple Chess Pie manages to be both exotic and traditional at the same time. The tropical flavors of pineapple and lime are enhanced by the richness of buttermilk and butter. Chess pie is a dessert with roots in the South and a name of uncertain derivation. (Suggestions run from a sort of cheese to the chest the pies were stored in.) Whatever the origins, chess pie holds a place in the hierarchy of traditional pies.

½ large extra-sweet pineapple, cleaned and sliced into ⅛-inch pieces, or one 20-ounce can drained pineapple pieces
½ cup (1 stick) butter, softened
⅔ cup confectioners' sugar
3 large eggs (room temperature)
¼ cup flour
½ cup buttermilk
1 teaspoon vinegar
2 tablespoons dark rum
2 teaspoons lime zest
1 teaspoon vanilla
½ recipe Perfect Pie Dough (p. 4), rolled and chilled for half an hour in a 9½-inch pie plate

PREHEAT THE OVEN TO 375°F.

In a medium bowl, whisk together the softened butter and the confectioners' sugar. Gradually whisk in the eggs one at a time. Stir in the flour, and gradually add the buttermilk, vinegar, dark rum, lime zest, and vanilla. Make sure the batter remains smooth as you incorporate the ingredients.

Blind bake the pie by first placing tinfoil over the raw dough and then filling it with pie weights or beans. Bake the well-rested pie shell in a 375°F oven for 15 to 20 minutes or until it appears dry. Place the chopped pineapple in the pie shell, and fill with the egg and buttermilk mixture. Turn the oven down to 350°F, and bake for 40 minutes or until the pie appears firm in the center.

PREPARING PINEAPPLE

To clean a pineapple, first cut off the bottom and the bushy top of the fruit. Stand the fruit on its flat bottom, and cut off all the skin on the sides of the fruit. Cut deep enough to remove all the eyes in the fruit. Try to lose as little of the yellow flesh as possible, while getting off all the skin.

When all the skin has been removed, cut the fruit in half. Lay the half on its flat side and slice into ¼-inch slices. Cut the ¼-inch slices into 3 pieces.

PUMPKIN CHEESECAKE PIE

Makes one 3-inch-
deep cheesecake

For a twist that will liven up traditional pumpkin pie, add cream cheese and sour cream to your favorite pumpkin pie recipe. You will need a springform cheesecake pan for this recipe.

two 8-ounce packages cream cheese

⅔ cup sugar

3 eggs

one 8-ounce can solid-pack pumpkin

½ cup sour cream

2 tablespoons flour

2 tablespoons lemon juice

1 teaspoon cinnamon

1 teaspoon salt

2 teaspoons vanilla

1 tablespoon candied ginger, finely chopped

1 recipe prepared graham cracker Cookie Crust (p. 7), placed in a 9-inch springform pan, baked and cooled

PREHEAT THE OVEN TO 350°F.

Cream the cream cheese with the sugar and slowly add the eggs. If using an electric mixer, insert the paddle attachment. When the eggs have been incorporated, add the pumpkin and sour cream. When the sour cream and pumpkin have been thoroughly incorporated, add the flour, lemon juice, cinnamon, salt, vanilla, and candied ginger.

Press the cookie crust into the bottom of the cheesecake pan. Bake at 350°F for 5 minutes to set up the crust. Fill the mold with the cheesecake filling, and place on a baking sheet. Bake the pie for 50 to 55 minutes at 350°F, until the center starts to become firm and set. Do not overcook the pie because it will crack. Allow the pie to cool in the oven with the door ajar and the oven turned off. Keep the pie chilled in the refrigerator.

TRADITIONAL PUMPKIN PIE

For a more traditional pie, combine one 15-ounce can pumpkin puree, 1 can sweetened condensed milk, 4 eggs, 2 tablespoons flour, ¼ cup brown sugar, 1 teaspoon cinnamon, ½ teaspoon clove, and ½ teaspoon ginger. Bake in a prebaked pie shell for 40 minutes at 400°F.

44

SOUTHERN SWEET POTATO PIE

Two southern staples, sweet potatoes and pecans, collide in this rendition of an American classic.

4 eggs
¾ cup brown sugar
½ cup sugar
2 cups sweet potato, cooked and mashed
1½ cups half-and-half, warmed
¼ cup (½ stick) butter, melted
1 teaspoon cinnamon
½ teaspoon mace
½ teaspoon salt
1 teaspoon vanilla
1 cup pecans
1 recipe crumbs from Nectarine Blueberry Crisp (p. 86)
½ recipe prepared Perfect Pie Dough (p. 4), rolled and chilled for half an hour in a 9-inch pie plate

PREHEAT THE OVEN TO 375°F.

In a medium bowl, whisk the eggs together with the brown sugar and regular sugar. Stir in the sweet potatoes, and gently whisk in the warmed milk and melted butter. Season the batter with cinnamon, mace, salt, and vanilla.

Line the pie shell with an oiled piece of aluminum foil, and fill with pie weights. Bake the pie shell in a 375°F oven for 15 to 20 minutes or until it appears dry. Add the sweet potato mixture, and turn down the oven to 350°F. Bake for an additional 20 minutes.

When the pie begins to set up, cover the top of the pie with prepared crumbs and the pecans. Bake for an additional 20 minutes. When the crumbs have browned, test the pie with a knife. The blade should come out clean when inserted in the center.

PREPARING SWEET POTATOES

Cooking sweet potatoes is similar to baking any type of potato. Roast them until soft in a medium-hot oven for about an hour, or microwave the sweet potatoes wrapped in plastic for 8 to 12 minutes, depending on the strength of your microwave.

LIME DAIQUIRI CHIFFON PIE

Lime and rum liven up this traditional recipe for chiffon pie. If you purchase the cookie crust already prepared, you won't need the oven at all.

¼ cup cold water
1½ envelopes unflavored gelatin (1 tablespoon plus 1½ teaspoons gelatin)
1 cup milk
2 teaspoons cornstarch
¾ cup sugar
3 eggs, separated
¼ cup dark rum
½ cup fresh lime juice
1 teaspoon vanilla
2 teaspoons lime zest
¾ cup heavy cream, whipped
1 recipe prepared vanilla Cookie Crust (p. 7), baked and cooled

Empty the gelatin into a small cup filled with ¼ cup cold water. Allow the gelatin to hydrate.

In a small saucepan, warm the milk. Combine ½ cup of the sugar and 2 teaspoons of cornstarch in a small container. In a medium bowl, place the three egg yolks; reserve the whites in a separate cup. Whisk the sugar and cornstarch mixture into the egg yolks until the mixture is smooth.

Temper the warm milk into the egg yolk mixture by gradually adding the milk ¼ cup at a time. Return the milk mixture to the saucepan, and whisk continually over low heat until the mixture simmers and becomes thickened.

When the milk and eggs are thick, remove them from the heat and stir in the gelatin. Gelatin must never be simmered. When the lump of gelatin has completely dissolved, add the lime zest, lime juice, rum, and vanilla. Allow this daiquiri mixture to cool.

Whisk the egg whites in a clean dry bowl, either by hand or with a mixer. Gradually add the remaining ¼ cup of sugar, and whisk until smooth and glossy.

Fold together the cooled daiquiri mixture and the egg whites. Fold in the whipped cream. If you do not wait until the filling has cooled, it will melt your whipped cream, taking the volume out of the pie. Heap the filling into the pie shell, and allow it to set for several hours in the refrigerator. Garnish the pie with candied citrus zest, whipped cream, or chocolate shavings.

THE SECRET OF CITRUS ZEST

The most underutilized source of flavor in the home kitchen is the naturally occurring oils found in the skins of citrus fruits: oranges, lemons, and limes. Most box graters have a grate size for citrus fruits, and most gourmet stores carry rasps or zesters for citrus grating. Rasps from the hardware store work as well as gourmet store zesters do, and they are much less expensive.

AMISH VANILLA PIE

My uncle made several traditional pies for breakfast and for snacking in the afternoon with coffee. Amish Vanilla Pie is one such pie. It has the traditional gooey bottom of the famous Pennsylvania Dutch shoofly pie, a sticky molasses-bottomed pie.

2 eggs
¼ cup sugar
¼ cup light brown sugar
2 tablespoons flour
½ cup molasses
1 cup milk
2 teaspoons vanilla
½ recipe prepared Perfect Pie Dough (p. 4), rolled and chilled for half an hour in a 9-inch pie plate
1 recipe Amish Crumb Topping (see below)

PREHEAT THE OVEN TO 375°F.

Combine the eggs, sugars, and flour in a medium bowl. Warm the milk and molasses in a medium saucepan. After the milk simmers, combine it gradually with the egg mixture.

Return the milk with the egg to the stove, and bring to a gentle simmer. Remove the pan from the heat, and stir in vanilla. Allow the mixture to cool.

Carefully crimp the edge of the pie shell, and fill the prepared pie shell with the vanilla pie filling. Sprinkle crumbs on top of the filling until it is very well covered. Bake at 375°F for 40 minutes. The pie is finished when the filling is firm and the crumbs brown.

amish crumb topping

Mix 1 cup of flour, 1 teaspoon baking powder, ½ teaspoon salt, ½ teaspoon cinnamon, and ¾ cup light brown sugar with ⅓ cup of butter. Sprinkle over the pie filling, and bake as directed.

SOUR CREAM RAISIN PIE

Makes one
9½-inch pie

A solid Midwestern classic, Sour Cream Raisin Pie uses ingredients readily available.

¾ cup water
¾ cup raisins
2 eggs
¾ cup brown sugar
½ teaspoon salt
1 teaspoon cinnamon
2 tablespoons flour
1⅓ cups sour cream
1 teaspoon vanilla
1 recipe Meringue Topping (p. 40)
½ recipe prepared Perfect Pie Dough (p. 4), blind baked and cooled

Bring water to a simmer and pour it over the raisins in a small cup. Allow the raisins to sit in the water overnight or until they become soft. When you are ready to use them, drain off the water and squeeze them to remove the excess liquid.

PREHEAT THE OVEN TO 350°F.

Combine the eggs and brown sugar in a medium bowl. Fold in the dry ingredients. When that mixture is well combined, add the sour cream, soft raisins, and vanilla. Place the filling in the prebaked pie shell, and bake for an additional 40 minutes at 350°F.

Make the meringue topping as described in the recipe for Mile-High Lemon Meringue Pie (p. 40).

After the sour cream filling has set up and is still hot, apply the meringue, and cook at 350°F until golden brown.

MORE ON MERINGUE

Meringue topping can be flavored with a spice like cinnamon or clove or a zest of lemon or orange. Other flavorings include extracts such as rum or almond. If you feel a little daring or want to create a special-occasion pie, put in a drop of food coloring, like green for St. Patrick's Day.

chocolate pies

CHOCOLATE CANDY BAR PIE	55
CHOCOLATE LEMON CHESS PIE	57
FUDGE BROWNIE PIE	59
CHOCOLATE CREAM CHEESE PEAKS	60
FRENCH SILK PIE WITH RASPBERRIES	62
BLACK BOTTOM CHIFFON PIE	63
FROZEN PEANUT BUTTER MOUSSE PIE	65
MISSISSIPPI MUD ICE CREAM PIE	67
MINI MOLTEN PIES	68

I have dedicated a chapter to chocolate pies for two reasons. First, people are passionate about chocolate. You are either addicted to it or unmoved by it. But if you got to have it, you got to have it.

Second, chocolate is a fascinating medium with which to cook. Rock hard when it is cold and a liquid when warm, its possibilities for creation are endless. Melted candy bars create a fluffy mousse in a Chocolate Candy Bar Pie, and the firmness of chilled chocolate combined with eggs creates a silky smooth French Silk Pie with Raspberries. The texture of a chocolate pie can range from a dense Fudge Brownie Pie to a frozen Mississippi Mud Ice Cream Pie, but the flavor remains delicious.

CHOCOLATE CANDY BAR PIE

Kids love this chocolate pie and can even help make it. Use your favorite chocolate for the filling and your favorite candy bar as garnish.

8 ounces semisweet chocolate
2 tablespoons butter
⅔ cup milk
2½ cups minimarshmallows (reserve ½ cup for garnish)
1 teaspoon salt
1 teaspoon vanilla
1 large bag Butterfingers candy bar miniatures
2 cups heavy cream, whipped
1 recipe prepared vanilla or chocolate Cookie Crust (p. 7), baked and cooled

Create a double boiler by placing a medium-sized bowl over a medium-sized saucepan of boiling water. Place the semisweet chocolate, butter, milk, marshmallows, salt, and vanilla in the bowl over the boiling water. Gently stir the ingredients until everything melts into smooth, liquid chocolate. Turn off the heat, and remove the bowl from the double boiler. Allow the mixture to cool. Put the bowl in the refrigerator for brief periods to speed the process along. Continually check the chocolate mixture while it is in the refrigerator, and keep stirring the chocolate to ensure it does not form any lumps.

Using the end of a rolling pin, smash 15 pieces of the Butterfinger candy bars in their wrappers. Empty the shards of candy into a small bowl, and put aside.

When the chocolate mixture is at room temperature, quickly fold in the first cup of heavy cream. Work quickly with a rubber spatula, and make certain all the lumps of chocolate and cream are completely incorporated. Fold in the second cup of whipped cream delicately. Keep the filling as light and fluffy as possible. Heap the mixture into a pie shell, and layer the filling with the crushed Butterfingers and ½ cup of minimarshmallows.

Smooth the mixture into the cookie crust. Using a decorative star tip, garnish the cake with any remaining chocolate mousse. Mousse for piping should not contain any whole marshmallows or candy since they would clog the piping tip. Use the remaining chocolate bars unwrapped as a garnish on your swirls of chocolate filling.

SHORTCUT

Make a quick, easy filling for your candy bar pie by melting 8 ounces of chocolate with 2 tablespoons of butter in a double boiler. While the chocolate is still hot, quickly fold in the whipped cream. Garnish the pie with candy bars, as in the recipe above.

CHOCOLATE LEMON CHESS PIE

The taste of good-quality bittersweet chocolate is enhanced by lemon zest. Serve this pie with candied lemon slices for added flavor.

⅔ cup sugar
4 eggs
1 tablespoon flour
½ cup butter, melted
3 ounces bittersweet chocolate, melted
1 cup half-and-half
juice of 1 lemon
2 teaspoons lemon zest
1 teaspoon vanilla
½ recipe prepared Perfect Pie Dough (p. 4), partially baked and warm

PREHEAT THE OVEN TO 375°F.

Melt the chocolate and butter together in a bowl over a pan or skillet of barely simmering water. In a medium bowl, whisk together the eggs and sugar. Whisk in the tablespoon of flour. Add the melted butter and chocolate into the eggs; mix until thoroughly combined. Slowly add the half-and-half, lemon juice, zest, and vanilla.

Line the pie with oiled tinfoil, and fill with pie weights. Bake the pie shell for 25 minutes at 375°F. Remove the pie from the oven, and fill the shell, while still warm, with the chocolate pie filling. Turn the oven temperature to 350°F. Bake for 30 to 40 minutes more, until the pie is set.

To prepare candied lemons, thinly slice three whole, rinsed lemons. Remove the seeds from the lemons to produce perfect lemon rounds. Lay the lemon rounds in a medium saucepan, and cover with cold water. Add 1 teaspoon of salt. Bring the cold water to a simmer, and cook the lemon rounds gently for about 10 to 15 minutes.

Carefully drain the water from the lemons. Refill the pot with enough water to cover the lemons, and simmer again. Change the water again, and bring lemons to a simmer one last time. Drain the lemons one final time, and return them to the pan. Do not add water after the final draining.

You should have about 1¼ to 1½ cups of lemons in the pot. On top of the lemons, pour 1¼ cups of sugar. Gently warm the lemon slices until the sugar begins to draw liquid from the lemons. Gradually, the lemons will become submerged in sugar syrup as their liquid is drawn out by the sugar. It is an amazing sight. When they are submerged, simmer the lemons for 5 minutes. Remove pot from the heat, and allow the lemons to come to room temperature in the syrup. To serve, scrape off excess syrup, and arrange decoratively across the pie, or dry the rounds overnight on a cake rack. Roll the lemons in sugar and eat as candy.

FUDGE BROWNIE PIE

Words can't describe the difference between this dense fudge brownie and that of a box mix brownie. This mix has no baking powder or leavening; it is essentially slow-cooked fudge filled with chocolate chips and nuts.

1 cup (2 sticks) butter
5 ounces unsweetened baking chocolate
5 eggs
2⅓ cups sugar
2 teaspoons vanilla
1 teaspoon salt
1 cup plus 4 tablespoons flour
1 cup white chocolate chips
1 cup walnuts, toasted (optional)
1 pint vanilla ice cream

PREHEAT THE OVEN TO 325°F.

Melt the chocolate and butter in a bowl over the top of a simmering pan or skillet of water.

In a large bowl, combine the eggs with the sugar, vanilla, and salt. Mix just to combine; do not overmix. Fold warm chocolate mixture into the just-combined eggs. Add the flour to the mixture, and stir until the flour is completely incorporated. Fold in the nuts and chocolate chips. Pour the batter into a 10-inch deep-dish pie plate.

Bake in a slow 325°F oven for 35 to 45 minutes, until the center is set and the edges are slightly raised. Cool the pie completely before cutting.

The market is full of brownie mixes that would suffice for a brownie pie, but there is something special about this combination. I like to cut the pie into thin wedges and balance two thin wedges between scoops of ice cream.

CHOCOLATE CREAM CHEESE PEAKS

A quick and easy no-bake pie, Chocolate Cream Cheese Peaks yields a sophisticated combination similar to a chocolate cheesecake.

8-ounce package cream cheese
½ cup brown sugar
3 tablespoons corn syrup
7 ounces semisweet chocolate, melted
½ teaspoon salt
1 teaspoon vanilla
1½ cups heavy cream, whipped with ¼ cup sugar
1 recipe prepared Cookie Crust (p. 7)
1 cup chocolate shavings, for garnish
½ cup confectioners' sugar, for garnish
1 recipe prepared Caramel Sauce (p. 61)

Make a double boiler by fitting a bowl on top of a saucepan of simmering water.

Melt the chocolate in the bowl, suspended above the barely simmering water. (Plain chocolate can also be melted in the microwave on medium power. Microwave the chocolate in 45-second increments. It should appear just melted in the center; stir it to dissolve any unmelted chocolate.)

Using the paddle attachment of a mixer, combine the cream cheese with brown sugar and corn syrup. Add the melted chocolate, salt, and vanilla. Keep the chocolate and cream cheese warm if you can't mix in the whipped cream immediately.

Quickly fold in half of the whipped cream until the mixture is smooth. Fold in the remainder of the whipped cream. Create dramatic swirled peaks by piping the pie filling into a cookie crust using a star tip. Chill the pie for at least 2 hours. Cover the pie with chocolate shavings, and sprinkle with confectioners' sugar.

caramel sauce

Caramel sauce is a delicious accompaniment to Chocolate Cream Cheese Peaks. Simply place ¼ cup water, ¼ cup corn syrup, and 1 cup sugar in a medium saucepan. Place the pan over medium heat, and cook until the sugar turns a dark amber color. Add ¼ cup of heavy cream, 3 tablespoons butter, and a pinch of salt to the saucepan; mix until the caramel is dissolved in the liquid. Chill and serve the sauce with the pie.

FRENCH SILK PIE WITH RASPBERRIES

Chocolaty and smooth, this French Silk Pie is elegant and easy. The texture is like soft, dense mousse; the flavor is like a raspberry truffle.

4 eggs
¾ cup sugar
6 ounces semisweet chocolate, chopped
¾ cup sweet butter (1½ sticks), at room temperature
½ teaspoon salt
2 tablespoons framboise (French raspberry liqueur) or vanilla extract
½ recipe prepared Perfect Pie Dough (p. 4), blind baked and cooled
1–2 pints raspberries
¼ cup confectioners' sugar

PREHEAT THE OVEN TO 375°F.

In a medium bowl, whisk the eggs and sugar. Create a double boiler by placing a bowl over a simmering pan of water. Warm the eggs over simmering water, whisking constantly. The eggs should be cooked between 140°F and 150°F. Use a candy thermometer or a meat thermometer to determine the temperature. Add the chocolate pieces and butter to the bowl over the double boiler, and stir until the mixture is completely smooth. Add the framboise or other fruit liqueur, such as Grand Marnier, to the chocolate. Pour the chocolate into the pie shell, and place the pie into the refrigerator to set up. When it is fully set, garnish the pie with a pile of raspberries. Sprinkle confectioners' sugar on top of the raspberries.

FLAVORED WHIPPED CREAM

Flavored whipped creams make a nice accompaniment to almost any pie. Flavor your whipped cream with any spice or extract or even instant coffee for a nice mocha cream. Small amounts of an alcohol, such as rum, or the zest of an orange might also be nice.

BLACK BOTTOM CHIFFON PIE

Light vanilla custard sits on top of soft chocolate ganache in a chocolate cookie crust in this rendition of a southern classic.

½ cup half-and-half
2 tablespoons butter
4 ounces bittersweet chocolate, chopped fine
1 tablespoon dark rum
1 recipe prepared chocolate Cookie Crust (p. 7), baked and cooled
2 cups milk
1¼ cups sugar
1½ tablespoons cornstarch
4 eggs, separated
⅛ teaspoon salt
1 teaspoon vanilla
1 cup heavy cream, whipped, for garnish
chocolate curls

Start by preparing the black bottom. In a small saucepan, bring the half-and-half and butter to a simmer. Place the bittersweet chocolate in a small bowl, and pour the simmering liquid over the chocolate. Stir gently until the chocolate and the liquid are thoroughly combined; then add the rum. Pour the mixture into the cookie crust, and allow the chocolate to set.

In a medium saucepan, warm the milk with ½ cup of sugar until it begins to simmer. In a small bowl, place the 4 egg yolks, reserving the whites for later. Combine the cornstarch with another ½ cup of the sugar and whisk into the yolks. Temper the yolks with the milk by slowly adding ¼ cup of the hot liquid at a time. Return the entire mixture to the saucepan when tempered, and simmer until thickened, stirring constantly. Add the vanilla, and remove the mixture from the heat.

Whisk the 4 egg whites with the salt, and gradually add the remaining ¼ cup of sugar. When the whites are firm and glossy, stop whisking and gently fold them into the vanilla custard. Allow the custard to cool slightly, and pour into the chocolate pie shell. Place the pie in the refrigerator, and let it cool completely. Garnish with whipped cream and chocolate curls.

Note: The consumption of raw egg is not recommended for everyone.

CHOCOLATE CURLS

To make decorative chocolate curls, you will need a bar of semisweet chocolate and a vegetable peeler. The chocolate should be the temperature of a warm room, but not near melting. Peel the chocolate with a vegetable peeler. Chocolate curls should peel off. If the chocolate cracks, it is too cold and can be warmed by putting it near a heat source or by rubbing it gently between your hands.

i ♥ pies and tarts

FROZEN PEANUT BUTTER MOUSSE PIE

Makes 1 heaping
10-inch pie

You and your children will love this frozen peanut butter cup. It is also my mother's favorite pie.

¾ cup crunchy peanut butter
¾ cup milk
½ teaspoon salt
¼ cup light corn syrup
½ cup sugar
2 cups heavy cream, whipped
1 recipe prepared chocolate Cookie Crust (p. 7), baked and cooled
1 recipe Chocolate Fudge Topping (p. 66)

In a medium bowl, whisk together the peanut butter and half of the milk. When the mixture is smooth, add the remaining milk. Blend the corn syrup and salt into the smooth peanut butter mixture.

Whisk the heavy cream while slowly adding the sugar. Make sure the cream stays chilled at all times.

Incorporate ⅓ of the whipped cream into the peanut butter mixture and stir until smooth. Gently fold in the remaining cream, keeping the mixture as light as possible.

Immediately transfer this mousse mixture into the cookie shell, smoothing the top. Place the pie in the coldest area of the freezer, and allow it to set for several hours.

When the pie is firmly set, melt the fudge topping until it is a liquid, but not hot. Spread the topping evenly over the pie, and return it to the freezer. Garnish with additional whipped cream and your favorite chocolate covered peanut candy, if desired.

chocolate fudge topping

Spread this chocolate fudge topping on any dessert for an elegant finish. In a double boiler over gently simmering water, melt 8 ounces of bittersweet chocolate with ¼ cup of butter, ⅓ cup of heavy cream, and 4 tablespoons of light corn syrup. Mix thoroughly until the topping is shiny and smooth. Allow the topping to become cool; remelt it when ready to use.

MISSISSIPPI MUD ICE CREAM PIE

Mississippi Mud Pie, a large, gooey, frozen ice cream dessert, is a treat at any time of the year. Layers of coffee ice cream, vanilla ice cream, and chocolate ice cream create a dramatic presentation.

1 pint coffee ice cream, softened
1 pint vanilla ice cream, softened
1 pint chocolate ice cream, softened
2 recipes prepared Chocolate Fudge Topping (from Frozen Peanut Butter Mousse Pie, p. 66)
¼ cup bourbon (added to the Chocolate Fudge Topping)
1 cup pecan pieces, toasted
1 recipe prepared chocolate Cookie Crust (p. 7), baked and cooled
1 cup heavy cream, whipped, for garnish

Soften the ice creams in the refrigerator one at a time, so the pie has time to set up between the constructing of the different layers. To soften the ice cream, place each container in the refrigerator for half an hour to 1 hour before using. Place a stainless-steel bowl in the freezer to chill. Dump the softened coffee ice cream into the chilled bowl, and mix until it becomes smooth. Add to the pie shell, and cover with a thin layer of room-temperature Chocolate Fudge Topping. Place the pie in the freezer.

Repeat the above process, using the other two flavors for layers two and three, adding a layer of Chocolate Fudge Topping between each ice cream flavor. Cover the top of the pie with the Chocolate Fudge Topping, and sprinkle it with toasted almonds. Freeze for several hours or overnight. Remove the pie from the freezer half an hour before serving, and garnish with whipped cream.

Frozen pies are convenient, and the flavor options are varied. Choose two or three contrasting ice creams, either complementary flavors or dramatically different colors, and create a signature pie of your own. Combine mint chocolate chip with raspberry and chocolate, or lime sherbet with vanilla ice cream and orange sherbet.

MINI MOLTEN PIES

A new American classic, the molten chocolate cake, has been translated into a bite-sized pie. The center remains gooey and soft while the outside is crusty and delicious. You will need special 2- to 4-inch tart molds for your minipies.

5 ounces chocolate, melted
2 tablespoons butter, melted
2 eggs, separated
¼ cup sugar
3 tablespoons flour
½ cup chopped almonds
1 recipe regular or chocolate Sweet Tart Dough (p. 8), baked in 2- to 4-inch molds

PREHEAT THE OVEN TO 350°F.

Line individual tart molds with tart dough. Allow them to set up in the refrigerator. Line the tarts with tinfoil, and fill with pie weights. Bake them at 350°F for 15 minutes, remove the tinfoil, and finish baking until they turn a light tan.

Melt the butter and chocolate in the top of a double boiler or in a bowl fitted over a pan or skillet of barely simmering water.

In a small bowl, whisk the egg yolks with half the amount of sugar and the flour. Fold the egg yolks and nuts into the chocolate mixture.

Whisk the egg whites in a clean, dry bowl. When they start to become stiff, add the remaining sugar. Fold the egg whites into the chocolate mix. Place enough batter into each tart shell to fill it a little more than level.

Bake in the 350°F oven for 8 to 10 minutes for 2-inch tarts and 12 to 15 minutes for 4-inch tarts. You will need to test a tart or two to perfect your technique. Baking times vary for different ovens. Serve warm if possible.

notes

rustic desserts

INDIVIDUAL FIG CROSTATAS 73

PEAR GALETTE 75

PENNSYLVANIA DUTCH APPLE DUMPLINGS 76

INDIVIDUAL APRICOT CHERRY FRIED PIES 78

MIXED BERRY TURNOVERS 80

SIMPLE VELVET CUSTARD PIE 82

HANDKERCHIEF APPLE PIE 84

NECTARINE BLUEBERRY CRISP 86

DEEP-DISH PLUM COBBLER 88

Rustic desserts are sexy. Instead of making a piece of fruit conform to a pie plate, the pie dough is configured to accommodate the fruit. Dough is wrapped around a serving of figs and baked for an Individual Fig Crostata. Dough is wrapped around a stuffed apple to create a Pennsylvania Dutch Apple Dumpling. The preparations require no special equipment or training. Baked fruit fillings are accented simply with honey, cheese, or nuts. The desserts are inspired by traditional preparations from the countrysides of Europe and America—simple, honest, and delicious.

INDIVIDUAL FIG CROSTATAS

Makes 8 to 10
individual tarts

Black mission figs are wrapped with sweet tart dough and finished with honey to create these free-form individual fig tarts. To help hold the tart together, I've added a touch of almond cream.

½ cup (1 stick) butter
⅔ cup sugar
1 cup almond flour (powdered almonds)
2 eggs
¼ cup flour
⅔ cup honey
2 quarts black mission figs, quartered, with stems removed
1 recipe Sweet Tart Dough (p. 8), rolled to ⅛ inch thick and chilled

PREHEAT THE OVEN TO 350°F.

Prepare a frangipane (an almond cream): In a medium bowl, cream the butter with the sugar. Add the almond flour to the bowl, and continue creaming until the contents are smooth. Gradually incorporate the eggs, adding them one at a time. Finish the recipe by folding in the flour.

Using a large ring-shaped cutter or a coffee saucer as a guide, cut the dough into 6-inch rounds. Place 2 tablespoons of frangipane in the center of each round of dough. Press 8 to 10 fig quarters into the frangipane. Slowly work your way around the tart, making loose pleats in the dough until the figs are wrapped in the dough. Place the crostatas on a sheet tray a few inches apart. They will not spread much.

Bake your little crostatas in a 350°F oven for 20 to 30 minutes. The crostadas are done when the crust is golden brown and the figs are brown on the edges.

Drizzle the tarts with honey, and serve warm.

The possibilities for different crostatas are virtually endless. Any fresh, ripe fruit from apples, pears, and peaches to grapes, nuts, and cheese makes delicious and simple tarts. Try pears and walnuts, and finish it with a little mascarpone, a mild Italian cow cheese, for a different treat.

PEAR GALETTE

Makes 1
free-form pie

The Pear Galette is a simple and sexy tart that requires no more effort than it takes to wrap dough around pears.

4 pears, peeled, cored, and thinly sliced
2 tablespoons flour
½ teaspoon salt
½ cup sugar
½ cup dried, sweetened cranberries
3 tablespoons butter
1 recipe Sweet Tart Dough (p. 8), rolled to ⅛ inch thick and chilled

PREHEAT THE OVEN TO 350°F.

Toss the pears with the flour, sugar, and salt in a medium bowl. When the dry ingredients have been completely combined, add the cranberries.

Cut the rolled tart dough into a round approximately 12 inches in diameter. Use either the lid of a pot or a dinner plate (the average dinner plate is 9 to 10 inches), and trace around the outside of your plate until you have a rough circle. It does not need to be perfect. Begin pleating the dough about every inch, and working your way around the tart, create a lip of dough around the edge. Place the dough on a flat sheet tray or inside a cake pan or tart ring for extra support. Fill the center hole created by the pleat with the pear filling; make sure the filling stays in the center cavity. Dot the filling with butter.

Bake in a 350°F oven for 40 to 45 minutes. The galette is finished when a knife passes easily through the pears and the crust is a rich brown.

PENNSYLVANIA DUTCH APPLE DUMPLINGS

My grandmother made these generous apple dumplings as an afternoon snack. They were a little too large for an ordinary dessert, unless you were having just a salad for dinner. She would put a warm dumpling in a small bowl and surround the pastry with cold milk. I have used her special recipe for the dough, which is wrapped around a whole apple like a present.

3 cups flour
1 teaspoon salt
½ cup (1 stick) butter
½ cup shortening
1 egg
¼ cup cold milk
1 tablespoon vinegar
8 medium apples, peeled and cored
4 tablespoons butter
1 recipe Filling for Dumplings (p. 77)

PREHEAT THE OVEN TO 350°F.

In a medium bowl, combine flour and salt. Cut in shortening and butter, using a mixer with a flat paddle attachment, or cut in by hand with a knife. When the mixture resembles wet sand, add the egg and vinegar. Splash in the milk, and mix the dough until it forms a smooth, pliable ball. Wrap the dough in plastic, and allow it to rest in the refrigerator for 20 minutes.

Roll out the dough on a lightly floured surface. The dough should be no more than ⅛ inch thick. Place an apple on the dough, and cut out a shape that can be folded up and sealed at the top to completely enclose the apple. Before covering the apple with dough, fill its center, where the core was removed, with the filling for dumplings that follows. Dab the top of the apple with a piece of butter. Seal the dough around the apple.

Bake for 50 minutes in a 350°F oven. When fully cooked, a knife should pass easily through the apple. Serve warm in a bowl with ice-cold milk or vanilla ice cream.

filling for dumplings

I like to make the traditional apple dumplings with this filling in the center. It creates a little surprise when you eat through the apple. Combine ½ cup light brown sugar, 4 tablespoons flour, 1 teaspoon cinnamon, ¾ cup dried cherries, and ¾ cup walnut pieces. In a plastic bag, crush the walnuts gently and toss with the rest of the ingredients. The filling is ready to be stuffed into the apples.

INDIVIDUAL APRICOT CHERRY FRIED PIES

A good late fall dessert, Apricot Cherry Fried Pies rely on dried fruit for the filling. Softened apricots and cherries are quickly fried, cooking the dough and warming the filling.

1 cup dried apricots
½ cup dried tart cherries
4 tablespoons rum
¼ cup sugar
2 teaspoons flour
¼ teaspoon salt
1 recipe Cream Cheese Pie Dough (p. 6), rolled out in a large square, ⅛ inch thick and chilled
1 cup confectioners' sugar
peanut oil for frying

In a small saucepan, combine the apricots and cherries. Add water until the fruit is just barely covered. Bring to a simmer, and let simmer for 2 to 3 minutes. Remove the pan from the heat, and allow the fruit to cool slowly. Drain off any excess liquid when the fruit reaches room temperature. Stir rum into the fruit. If possible, allow the fruit to hydrate overnight or for a few hours.

When you are ready to make the pies, combine the dried fruit with the flour, salt, and sugar.

Cut 4-inch circles out of the rested pie dough. Place a generous spoonful of fruit into the center of each circle. Dab water around the edge of the dough using a pastry brush. Seal the edges tightly by crimping with a fork. Place the pies in the refrigerator and allow them to set up for 30 minutes.

Heat peanut oil to 350°F in a fryer or large pot. Submerge pies in oil a few at a time, taking care to not overcrowd the pan. When they turn golden brown on both sides, place the pies on paper towels to drain excess oil. Sprinkle the pies with confectioners' sugar and serve immediately.

It's no secret why fried pies are so delicious—they are always fresh. A fried pie is cooked in the few minutes before it is served and is still warm from the fryer. Wait until the last possible minute to cook your pie, then serve it hot after rolling it in confectioners' sugar.

MIXED BERRY TURNOVERS

I like to use Cream Cheese Pie Dough for these delicious little turnovers. Any combination of seasonal berries will work.

1 pint blueberries
1 pint blackberries
1 pint raspberries
2½ tablespoons quick-cooking tapioca
½ cup sugar
1 tablespoon lemon juice
1 recipe Cream Cheese Pie Dough (p. 6), rolled to ⅛ inch thick and chilled for half an hour
1 egg, for egg wash

PREHEAT THE OVEN TO 350°F.

In a large bowl, toss the blueberries with the tapioca, sugar, and lemon juice. Allow the berries to sit for 15 minutes. In a small saucepan, bring the blueberries to a gentle simmer for several minutes. Remove the pan from the heat and stir in the blackberries and the raspberries. Allow the mixture to cool completely.

Using a pastry wheel, cut 4-inch squares of dough and refrigerate. Place ¼ cup of berry filling in each turnover, and seal the edges of the turnover with water. Cut three slits through the tops of the turnovers, and allow them to rest for a few minutes.

Whisk an egg with a few tablespoons of water. Brush the turnovers with the egg wash.

Bake for 25 minutes in a 350°F oven. The turnovers are done when they turn golden brown and bubble with juice.

APPLE TURNOVERS

To make apple turnovers, peel, core, and dice 6 apples. In a saucepan with 2 tablespoons of butter, a small handful of sugar, cinnamon, and salt, cook the apples until they are soft. Allow the filling to cool, and make it into turnovers using the method described above.

SIMPLE VELVET CUSTARD PIE

When simple is best, make a Velvet Custard Pie. The texture of this pie is like smooth, old-fashioned cup custard with a buttery crust.

2½ cups milk
3 tablespoons butter, melted
5 eggs
⅔ cup sugar
1 teaspoon salt
1 teaspoon nutmeg
2 teaspoons vanilla
½ recipe prepared Perfect Pie Dough (p. 4), baked and warm

PREHEAT THE OVEN TO 375°F.

Bake the pie in a preheated 375°F oven for 20 minutes. Remove the pie from the oven, and take out the tinfoil and weights. Turn the oven down to 350°F, return the pie to the oven, and bake until the pie shell is a light golden brown.

While the pie shell is baking, warm the milk in a medium saucepan with the butter. In a medium bowl, whisk together the eggs, sugar, salt, nutmeg, and vanilla. While whisking the eggs, pour the milk and melted butter in a steady stream into the egg mixture. Whisk continually until the mixture is well combined.

Return the pie shell to the oven, and slowly pour the warm custard mixture into the shell. Bake the pie for 20 minutes at 350°F or until the filling appears firm when gently shaken. Overcooking will make the pie taste like egg and the custard will be rubbery, so bake until just set.

To avoid a soggy crust, bake an empty pie shell until it appears golden and dry. When possible, add the liquid filling while both the liquid and the pie shell are still hot. The quicker the filling sets up, the drier the crust will be.

HANDKERCHIEF APPLE PIE

Makes one
10-inch pie

The extravagant presentation of the Handkerchief Apple Pie makes it a "wow" at any dinner party. The relatively quick and easy preparation makes it a "wow" for the cook. Prepared phyllo dough is layered in a pie plate, filled with apples, and covered with a shower of phyllo handkerchiefs.

6 tart apples, peeled, cored, and sliced into ¼-inch wedges
2 tablespoons lemon juice
½ cup sugar
2 tablespoons flour
1 teaspoon cinnamon
½ teaspoon salt
1 cup (2 sticks) butter, melted
1 cup confectioners' sugar, placed in a shaker or dry sieve
one 16-ounce package of prepared phyllo dough, defrosted and brought to room temperature

PREHEAT THE OVEN TO 325°F.

In a large bowl, sprinkle the prepared apples with the lemon juice. In a separate small bowl, combine the sugar, flour, cinnamon, and salt. Toss the dry ingredients with the apples until well mixed.

Working with phyllo dough is a fairly simple task, yet it requires a quick hand because the dough tends to dry out rather quickly. To give yourself more time to work, lay the dough out flat on your counter and cover it with a towel that is slightly damp. To remove a sheet, peel back the towel, take a sheet, and cover the remaining dough with the towel again.

Create your phyllo pie in a deep dish with steep sides for the best results. Begin by brushing the first piece of phyllo dough with melted butter. A pastry brush is recommended for this task. Sprinkle the dough liberally with confectioners' sugar, and drape it over one edge of the pie plate, allowing the remainder of the dough to fill in a section of the bottom of the pie plate. Repeat the buttering and sugaring of the dough as you work your way around the pie plate. Five sheets of dough should cover all the edges of the plate as well as overlap. Place another layer of phyllo sheets on top of the first, taking care to overlap the dough and evenly cover the pie plate. Keep layering the dough until you have about 20 sheets of dough overlapping in the plate. This procedure creates a crust.

Fill the pie with the prepared apple filling. When the pie is filled, wrap the loose ends of phyllo onto the top of the pie. Lay 5 sheets of buttered and sugared dough loosely over the top to cover the ends of the shell, and cover the top. The pie should appear to have dramatic handkerchiefs of dough on top. Bake the pie in a 325°F oven for about 60 minutes. Sprinkle the finished pie with additional confectioners' sugar and serve.

Phyllo lends itself to many presentations, from strudel to phyllo cups. The dough will hold any shape to which it is configured; just be sure to butter and sugar it. If you have never worked with phyllo, buy some in the freezer section, defrost it, and begin to create.

NECTARINE BLUEBERRY CRISP

A warm Nectarine Blueberry Crisp with ice cream on a summer night is as good as the simple life gets. Ripe seasonal fruit warmed with a covering of crisp crumbs is almost impossible to stop eating.

2 pints blueberries, cleaned and stems removed

6 ripe nectarines, peeled and pitted, sliced into ½-inch wedges

4 tablespoons quick-cooking tapioca

¾ cup sugar

3 tablespoons lemon juice

topping

2 cups flour

1 teaspoon cinnamon

1 teaspoon salt

⅓ cup sugar

⅓ cup brown sugar

½ cup (1 stick) butter

1¼ cups almonds, coarsely chopped

PREHEAT THE OVEN TO 350°F.

In a medium bowl, combine the nectarines and blueberries. Toss the fruit with sugar, lemon juice, and tapioca. Set the fruit aside while you prepare the crumbs.

Combine flour, cinnamon, salt, and sugars in a small bowl. Incorporate the butter into the dry ingredients. When the mixture forms clumps, stir in the almonds. The recipe will easily work without almonds, if you don't want to use them.

Bake the crisp in a 350°F oven for 50 minutes, until the fruit bubbles slowly and the crumbs on top become cooked and crisp.

In the summer, when my family was away on a trip and there was not much space to carry lots of ingredients, my mother would take a box of yellow cake mix and combine it with ½ cup (1 stick) of butter to make the crumbs. Then all she would need to prepare would be the fruit.

DEEP-DISH PLUM COBBLER

Makes one 2- to
3-quart casserole

Buttermilk biscuit dough dotted with butter and sugar form a topping for this crustless plum pie. The cobbler should be prepared in a deep, square, straight-sided casserole dish with flaky sweet biscuits baked on top.

filling

2–3 pounds ripe plums, stones removed and sliced into ½-inch wedges

2 tablespoons lemon juice

¾ cup sugar

½ teaspoon salt

¼ cup quick-cooking tapioca

biscuits

2 cups flour

1 teaspoon salt

2 teaspoons baking powder

½ teaspoon baking soda

6 tablespoons sugar

½ cup vegetable shortening

½ cup plus 4 tablespoons buttermilk

3 tablespoons butter

PREHEAT THE OVEN TO 350°F.

In a large bowl, toss the prepared plums with the lemon juice. Combine ¾ cup of sugar with the salt and tapioca, and then toss the mixture with the plums. Set this mixture aside.

i ♥ pies and tarts

In a separate mixing bowl, prepare the biscuits. Combine the flour, salt, baking powder, baking soda, and 3 tablespoons of sugar. Add the vegetable shortening to the bowl, and combine it with the flour mixture, using your mixer with a paddle attachment or combining by hand using a knife. When the mixture resembles coarse sand, add the buttermilk. As soon as the dough begins to pull together, turn off the mixer (if using) and finish kneading the dough by hand.

Lightly grease a 2-quart casserole dish, preferably one that is square with 2- to 3-inch sides, and fill with the plum mixture. Break off cobbler dough into small knobs, and cover plums completely. Dot the biscuit dough with butter, and sprinkle with the remaining 3 tablespoons of sugar. Bake for 35 to 45 minutes at 350°F, until the filling bubbles and the biscuit dough is browned.

SHORTCUT

For a simple homemade dessert, grease your casserole dish lightly and fill with tart cherry pie filling. Using a prepared tube of buttermilk biscuit dough from the grocery store, dot the filling with the dough. Sprinkle the dough with sugar and bake for 15 to 20 minutes at 350°F.

notes

sophisticated tarts

APRICOT FRANGIPANE TART	93
WALNUT CARAMEL TART	94
RASPBERRY JAM TART	96
CLAFOUTIS CHERRY CUSTARD TART	98
FRESH BERRY TART	99
CRANBERRY ALMOND TART	101
LEMON CURD TARTLETS	103
DOUBLE CHOCOLATE GANACHE TARTS	105

The European-inspired tart can be distinguished from a casual pie by its low, straight-sided, usually fluted crust. The dough for the crust is a crisp and crumbly sugar cookie texture, instead of the flaky and tender crust of a pie. Usually quite thin, a tart showcases the beautiful fruit or nut filling arranged inside. Special tart pans are needed, and those with removable bottoms are recommended.

APRICOT FRANGIPANE TART

Apricot Frangipane Tart is a traditional tart combination of almonds and apricots. Fresh apricots are sometimes hard to find, so I frequently use canned apricots. When baked in the almond cream, canned apricots are usually comparable to fresh.

½ cup butter
⅔ cup sugar
1 cup almond flour (powdered almonds)
2 eggs
¼ cup flour
two 12-ounce cans apricot halves, drained and patted dry, or 15 fresh, medium-sized apricots, pitted and halved
¼ cup apricot jam
1 recipe prepared almond Sweet Tart Dough (p. 8), chilled and rested in a tart pan

PREHEAT THE OVEN TO 350°F.

First, make the frangipane (FRAN-juh-pain). In a medium bowl, cream the butter with the sugar. Add the almond flour to the bowl and continue creaming. Gradually incorporate the eggs, adding them one at a time. Finish the recipe by folding in the flour.

Using a spoon, cover the bottom of the tart shell with almond cream to a depth of about ¼ inch. Arrange the apricots, cut side down, in the almond cream. Bake in a preheated oven for 60 to 70 minutes at 350°F, until the frangipane is golden brown and springs back when touched.

Warm the apricot jam in a small saucepan on the stove. Thin the jam with a few tablespoons of water, and use a pastry brush to apply the jam to the tart.

Frangipane is useful in the pastry kitchen; it can be used to fill many kinds of tarts, including jam tart and pear tart. Frangipane basically forms a protective barrier that keeps the crust from getting too soggy.

WALNUT CARAMEL TART

Walnut caramel tart is a good, sweet tart to serve for an afternoon snack. The straightforward, honest flavor goes great with a strong cup of coffee.

1 cup sugar
⅓ cup light corn syrup
6 tablespoons butter
⅔ cup heavy cream
2 teaspoons instant coffee
2 tablespoons rum
2½ cups walnut halves, lightly toasted
1 recipe prepared Sweet Tart Dough (p. 8), blind baked and warm

PREHEAT THE OVEN TO 325°F.

In a heavy saucepan, combine the sugar and corn syrup with enough water to make a texture like wet sand. Bring the mixture to a boil, and cook until the sugars turn an amber caramel color. If you don't make caramel frequently, remove the pan from the stove when the mixture reaches a light- to medium-caramel color. Carryover cooking will continue to darken the caramel without additional heat. In the following order, stir in butter, heavy cream, instant coffee, and rum. The mixture will bubble and splatter when you add the butter, so be careful to stand back.

Stir in lightly toasted walnuts, and pour the filling into a tart shell that has been completely baked. Smooth the filling to make it even, and place the tart in a 325°F oven for 10 minutes. Allow the tart to cool completely and serve.

CHOCOLATE WHIPPED CREAM

The perfect accompaniment to a walnut tart is a small scoop of mousse-like chocolate whipped cream. To make chocolate whipped cream, bring 1 cup of heavy cream to a boil. Pour it over 5½ ounces of chopped milk chocolate. Wait 1 minute, and then stir the mixture together. Chill the chocolate well, preferably overnight. Whisk the chocolate cream with a small whisk when needed, scoop it onto the tart, and serve.

RASPBERRY JAM TART

Makes one
10-inch tart

For this simple jam tart, I use special, spiced linzer dough. In addition to the dough, you will need a good-quality jam to finish your tart. Shape the dough into a tart of any size, or even a small cookie; use either a round or a rectangular tart pan.

½ cup (1 stick) butter
½ cup sugar
1⅔ cups flour
½ teaspoon cinnamon
⅔ cup almond flour (powdered almonds)
2 teaspoons cocoa powder
¼ teaspoon ground cloves
2 teaspoons lemon zest
2 eggs
1 cup good-quality raspberry jam
½ cup confectioners' sugar

PREHEAT THE OVEN TO 350°F.

Cream the butter and sugar in a mixing bowl, using the paddle attachment. Sift together the flour, cinnamon, almond flour, cocoa powder, and cloves. With the mixer on low, gradually add the dry ingredients to the butter and sugar. Finish the dough by adding the lemon zest and eggs, mixing just until the dough holds together. Wrap the dough and allow it to rest in the refrigerator for half an hour.

Lightly spray your tart pan to keep the dough from sticking. Roll the dough out to about ⅛ inch thick. Cut a piece of dough that will comfortably cover the pie tin and the sides of the tin. Work the dough into the bottom and up the sides of the pie tin. Generously spread the raspberry jam into the bottom

i ♥ pies and tarts

of the tart pan. Cut strips of dough to make a lattice on top of the tart. Bake in a 350°F oven for 30 to 40 minutes. Sprinkle the tart with the confectioners' sugar.

RASPBERRY SAUCE

Berries are available all year round. To make a quick and easy Raspberry Sauce to accompany your Raspberry Jam Tart, simply simmer 1 or 2 pints of raspberries (or strawberries) with ½ cup of sugar mixed with 2 teaspoons of cornstarch and a squeeze of lemon juice. If your berries are not juicy, add ½ cup of water and simmer. Strain out the seeds and stems and chill your sauce. Splash in 2 table-spoons of a fruit-flavored brandy, and your sauce is ready to serve.

CLAFOUTIS CHERRY CUSTARD TART

Clafoutis (kluh-foo-TEE) is a pancake-like tart traditionally served without a crust. Some flour is incorporated into the batter, thus giving it shape. Often you find it with a crust, to make handling easier. The choice is really yours; if you want to make it with a crust, use tart dough. French in origin, clafoutis is usually made with big, sweet cherries and baked in an earthenware tart shell.

2 eggs
⅔ cup sugar
2 cups half-and-half
1 cup pastry flour
⅛ teaspoon salt
1 teaspoon vanilla
1 tablespoon orange zest (optional)
2 tablespoons butter
2–3 cups sweet cherries, pitted and halved

PREHEAT THE OVEN TO 375°F.

In a small bowl, combine the eggs and sugar. Alternating between the half-and-half and the flour, gradually add these two ingredients. Finish the batter by adding the salt, vanilla, and orange zest.

Butter your tart pan and place fruit on the bottom. Put the pan in a preheated 375°F oven. When the pan is settled on a tray, slowly pour the batter to the rim of the tart pan. Bake for 20 minutes or until firm.

VARIATION

Even though cherry is the traditional filling for this tart, you may want to try this preparation with plums, apricots, or even sliced apples.

FRESH BERRY TART

The Fresh Berry Tart is a prebaked cornmeal tart shell filled with pastry cream and topped with fresh, ripe berries. Any ripe fruit that can be eaten without cooking can be used in this tart. The pastry cream can be flavored in a wide range of flavors, from orange and chocolate to mint and lavender. Feel free to create your own combination.

2 cups milk
⅔ cup sugar
2 eggs
½ cup flour
¼ teaspoon salt
1 teaspoon vanilla
4 tablespoons butter
1 pint raspberries
2 pints strawberries
1 pint blueberries
1 pint blackberries
1 recipe cornmeal Sweet Tart Dough (p. 8)
½ cup apricot jam

Carefully line a tart pan with the cornmeal tart dough. Allow the tart shell to set up in the freezer.

PREHEAT THE OVEN TO 400°F.

Oil a piece of tinfoil and press it into the tart shell to help support it. Pie weights or rice should be used to help support the tart sides. Cook the tart shell for 20 minutes at high heat, and then remove the tinfoil and finish baking the tart completely.

SOPHISTICATED TARTS

In a medium saucepan, bring milk to a simmer with a handful of the sugar. In a small container, combine the remaining sugar and salt with the flour. Place the eggs in a bowl and whisk the flour-sugar mixture into the eggs. The resulting mixture should be lump free. Gradually add the heated milk, whisking constantly. Return the milk and egg mixture to the stove, and whisk over very low heat. The milk should come to a simmer and slowly thicken. Remove the pastry cream from the heat; stir in vanilla and butter. Remove the pastry cream from the pot. Allow the cream to cool in the refrigerator with a piece of plastic wrap resting on its surface to keep a skin from forming.

Remove the tart shell from the pan, and fill it with the pastry cream. Arrange the fruit decoratively on top. Warm the apricot jam with a little water, and brush it over the fresh fruit to give it a nice shine.

FLAVORING PASTRY CREAM

Pastry cream is easily flavored with extracts. Incorporating a tablespoon or two of cocoa powder or a small piece of chocolate makes a delicious chocolate pastry cream. Infusing the milk with citrus zests, herbs, or nuts before making the cream is also a good way to create a more flavorful pastry cream.

CRANBERRY ALMOND TART

Makes one
10-inch tart

The Cranberry Almond Tart is a surprisingly delicious tart. Its rich, golden, honey caramel offsets the tartness of fresh cranberries. This colorful tart is a surprise ending to a Thanksgiving meal or any fall or winter gathering.

1 cup sugar
⅔ cup honey
6 tablespoons butter
½ cup heavy cream
1½ cups slivered almonds, roasted until golden
½ cup pistachios (optional)
1¼ cups fresh or frozen cranberries
1 recipe prepared Sweet Tart Dough (p. 8), fully baked and warm

PREHEAT THE OVEN TO 350°F.

In a medium saucepan, combine the sugar and honey with about ½ cup water to create a texture like wet sand. Bring the mixture to a simmer, and cook until it turns an amber-caramel color.

Remove the saucepan from the stove, and add the butter and heavy cream. Continue to stir the mixture, preferably with a wooden spoon. Add the almonds, pistachios, and cranberries. Stir the ingredients until well mixed.

Pour the filling from the saucepan into a prepared 1-inch tall tart pan. Smooth out the nuts and cranberries, arranging them evenly in the pan. Bake the tart for 20 to 25 minutes at 350°F. Allow the tart to cool completely before serving.

Every year around Thanksgiving, my grandmother would make mincemeat pies in the traditional fashion she remembered from her youth. She minced scraps of venison, that most plentiful Pennsylvania protein, and cooked the meat with a lot of sugar and spice to both preserve the meat and disguise any gamy flavor. She ate her mincemeat pie alone, even if it took her until Christmas to finish it. Nobody in the family would touch it. At restaurants, Grandmother grimaced when the waiters admitted their pies were made with beef, beef suet, or worse yet, just apples.

Old-fashioned preserving methods and the consumption of less-than-choice cuts of meat has long fallen out of fashion, making traditional mincemeat pies the product of a bygone era. In my grandmother's memory, I am leaving mock mincemeat pie out of the book. If you want a spicy apple pie with raisins, just call it a spicy apple pie with raisins.

LEMON CURD TARTLETS

I frequently put these lemon tartlets on restaurant menus, and their rich, dramatic lemon flavor and clean lines always make them a big seller. Lemon Curd Tartlets go well with fresh or slightly soured cream that has been whipped or frozen into an ice cream or sorbet. You will need twelve 3- to 4-inch small tartlet molds, or one 9-inch tart mold, to make this dessert.

3 eggs
3 yolks
1 cup sugar
1 teaspoon vanilla
¼ teaspoon salt
1 cup lemon juice
¾ cup (1½ sticks) butter
1 recipe prepared Sweet Tart Dough (p. 8), baked and warm

PREHEAT THE OVEN TO 350°F.

Line tartlet molds with dough, and cover the dough with a piece of tinfoil that has been lightly oiled. Weigh the tinfoil down with pie weights or uncooked rice or beans. Bake until they are fully cooked, 20 to 25 minutes. Remove them from the oven when done and take off the weights and tinfoil.

Create a double boiler by fitting a medium saucepan or widemouthed skillet, half filled with simmering water, with a medium bowl. Before placing the bowl over the water, combine all the ingredients.

Place the eggs and yolks in the bowl, and whisk in the sugar, vanilla, and salt. Slowly pour in the lemon juice. Place the bowl snugly on the saucepan, suspended over but not touching the water. Stir constantly while the mixture thickens, for about half an hour. When the mixture has thickened, remove it from the heat and stir in butter. Cool the lemon curd.

Preheat the oven to 450°F. Fill the precooked tart shells with the curd, and level them off with a knife. Place the tarts in a hot oven for 10 minutes, until the curd browns slightly on the rim of the tart. Remove the tarts from the oven, and allow them to set at room temperature.

Tart rings are bottomless ¼-inch-tall rings that are used to set up fragile tarts that can't be removed from tart pans with bottoms. You will have the best results with this tart if you use this type of ring. They should be available at gourmet cooking stores or on the Internet.

DOUBLE CHOCOLATE GANACHE TARTS

Makes 2 dozen mini
or 8 individual tarts

Melt-in-your-mouth chocolate ganache (guh-NASH) sits in a chocolate tart shell, creating a chocolate-on-chocolate dream. I usually make these tartlets bite-sized because they are so rich, but they can also be made in individual and large sizes.

1 cup heavy cream
8 ounces bittersweet chocolate, chopped fine
4 tablespoons orange liqueur, such as Grand Marnier or cointreau
candied orange peel for garnish
1 recipe chocolate Sweet Tart Dough (p. 8), baked in individual 1- to 3-inch molds or miniature tart molds

Place the chopped chocolate in a small bowl. Bring the cream to a simmer, and pour over the chopped chocolate. After letting the chocolate sit for a few minutes, stir the chocolate and cream with a rubber spatula. Incorporate the orange liqueur.

Allow the ganache to sit until it cools and thickens enough to work with. When stirred, it will begin to hold its shape for a few seconds before dissolving back into the bowl.

Pour the ganache into a pastry bag with a small tip or a cup with a spout—a measuring cup, for example—and slowly pour the ganache into the tart shells. Allow the tarts to set up at room temperature for several hours. Garnish with chopped candied orange peel.

Replace the orange liqueur with a drop or two of mint oil, available at cake specialty stores and gourmet shops. Make sure to get mint oil and not extract; there is a considerable difference between the two. Mix the mint oil with the ganache to make mint chocolate tartlets.

savory pies

SPINACH FETA PIE   109
QUICHE LORRAINE   111
CHEDDAR CHEESE CORN PIE   112
STEAK AND KIDNEY PIE   113
ONION GOAT CHEESE TART   115

Only in the United States does the mention of pie evoke thoughts of sweet fruity fillings and gooey nuts. In most of the world, meat pies—savory pies—are more the norm. Kidneys, beef, and cheese with vegetables are expected. Steak and Kidney Pie from England and a Greek-inspired Spinach Feta Pie are included in this section. Other favorites include brunch-inspired egg pies, like Quiche Lorraine and the French-style Onion Goat Cheese Tart.

SPINACH FETA PIE

This version of the Greek spanikopita (spinach pie) demonstrates the versatility of phyllo dough. The layers of paper-thin dough are brushed with butter and layered onto each other to create a flaky layer of dough on the top and the bottom of the pie. An 8-by-10-inch casserole dish at least 2 inches deep will be needed for this preparation.

4 bunches spinach, stems trimmed and washed three times, or three 10-ounce boxes of frozen spinach, thawed
3 tablespoons olive oil
1 yellow onion, thinly sliced
3 cloves garlic, mashed and chopped
4 eggs, lightly beaten
1 pound ricotta cheese
¾ pound feta cheese
1 tablespoon salt
2 teaspoons black pepper
one 16-ounce package phyllo dough
1 cup (2 sticks) butter, melted

Make certain to soak and thoroughly wash fresh spinach because it tends to be very muddy and sandy. Drain the spinach well, and dry in a salad spinner or with paper towels.

Warm the olive oil in a large sauté pan. Cook the yellow onion until it turns translucent. Add the garlic and continue to cook. The spinach can be added to the sauté pan two or three handfuls at a time and cooked until wilted. When the sauté pan is full, remove the contents and continue to wilt all the spinach. Frozen and thawed spinach does not need to be cooked.

In a medium bowl, lightly beat 4 eggs. Stir in the ricotta and feta cheeses, and season with salt and pepper. When the spinach has come to room temperature, add it to the egg-cheese mixture.

PREHEAT THE OVEN TO 350°F.

Unwrap the phyllo dough, and gently unroll it. Cover it with a lightly damp towel. Butter the sheets of phyllo one at a time, and layer them in your casserole dish so that they cover the bottom and sides of the dish. The phyllo should be eight layers deep all over the dish. Fill the dish with the cheese and spinach filling, and layer eight more pieces of phyllo over the top. Seal the dough around the edges with a little tuck to keep the filling from spilling out.

Bake the pie for 40 to 45 minutes in a 350°F oven. Cut the pie into individual pieces while warm; the pie is difficult to cut neatly when the phyllo is cold.

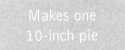

QUICHE LORRAINE

Quiche Lorraine is the quintessential brunch egg dish. Swiss cheese, bacon, and sometimes spinach are baked into custard for a filling morning meal or light dinner.

10 strips bacon
1 yellow onion, sliced into half-moons
2 pounds fresh spinach, stems removed, well-cleaned, and chopped
4 eggs
2 cups warmed milk
2 teaspoons salt
1 teaspoon black pepper
1 teaspoon nutmeg
1 cup Swiss cheese
½ recipe Savory Tart Dough (p. 10), blind baked

PREHEAT OVEN TO 400°F.

In a large sauté pan, cook the bacon until crisp. Drain the bacon on paper towels, and remove some of the grease from the sauté pan. Sauté the onions in the remaining grease until translucent. Stir in the spinach and leave the pan on the heat until spinach is wilted. Remove the vegetables from the hot pan.

In a medium bowl, whisk the eggs with the salt, pepper, and nutmeg. Add the warm milk in a slow stream. Mix the egg base well.

Crumble the bacon into the empty pie shell, and then add the onions and wilted spinach. Pour the egg mixture into the pie shell and place in a hot oven. Bake the quiche for 15 minutes, and then lower the temperature to 350°F for an additional 20 to 30 minutes.

Any combination of cheeses, breakfast meats, and vegetables can be used in the egg base to make a quiche.

CHEDDAR CHEESE CORN PIE

A little heat from chili peppers makes this savory pie a delicious change. Serve it with chicken or on its own.

2 tablespoons olive oil
1 yellow onion, sliced into half-moons
1 red pepper, thinly sliced
2 jalapeño peppers, seeds removed and finely chopped
1½ cups frozen corn or fresh corn cut from the cob
4 eggs
2 cups milk
2 teaspoons salt
½ teaspoon red pepper
1 cup sharp cheddar cheese, grated
1 cup diced ham
½ recipe Savory Tart Dough (p. 10), prebaked in a 10-inch pie plate

PREHEAT THE OVEN TO 350°F.

Warm 2 tablespoons of olive oil in a large sauté pan, and add the onions and red peppers to the pan. Cook the vegetables until they begin to soften and the onions become translucent. Add the corn and jalapeños to the pan, and continue to cook for another 5 minutes.

In a small saucepan, warm the milk. Break the eggs into a bowl, and season with salt and red pepper. When the milk begins to simmer, slowly add it to the egg mixture ¼ cup at a time.

Arrange the cooked vegetables, cheese, and ham in the prebaked pie shell, and place the pie shell on a sheet tray. Place the sheet tray in the preheated oven, and slowly pour the egg mixture into the pie. Bake for 30 to 40 minutes at 350°F.

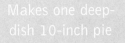
STEAK AND KIDNEY PIE

Steak and Kidney Pie is a traditional English preparation, a rich meat dish perfect for a chilly day. If kidneys are not to your liking, or are hard to obtain, substitute additional mushrooms or potatoes for the kidneys.

4 tablespoons (½ stick) butter
2 pounds round steak, cubed
¾ pound veal kidney, membrane and gristle removed and soaked in milk for at least 1 hour
¼ cup flour
1 tablespoon salt
2 teaspoons black pepper
1 yellow onion, sliced
2 cups domestic mushrooms, sliced
1 cup beef stock
1 cup red wine
1 tablespoon tomato paste
3 sprigs rosemary
4 sprigs thyme
1 recipe Perfect Pie Dough (p. 4), rolled and chilled for half an hour in a 10-inch pie plate

PREHEAT THE OVEN TO 350°F.

Heat a large sauté pan and warm 2 tablespoons of the butter until it bubbles. Dredge the meat and kidneys in flour, and brown all the meat in the skillet. Place the meat in a large pot with a lid. Sauté the onions and mushrooms in the last 2 tablespoons of butter. When they have finished cooking, place the vegetable in the pot. Deglaze the sauté pan with a little red wine, and empty the pan into the pot with the rest of the ingredients.

Add the remainder of the ingredients, including any leftover flour, to the pot. Let the pot simmer for at least 1 hour. When the gravy is thick, cool the meat and sauce.

Fill the rested pie dough with the cooled meat and filling. Cover with the second piece of dough, and cut vents for the steam to escape. Bake the pie at 350°F for 60 to 65 minutes.

ONION GOAT CHEESE TART

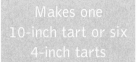

Makes one
10-inch tart or six
4-inch tarts

A French café favorite, Onion Goat Cheese Tart is a light late dinner with a glass of white wine or hearty lunch with a good salad.

2 tablespoons olive oil

1 teaspoon salt

3 sweet onions, such as Vidalia, thinly sliced

8 ounces mild goat cheese (fresh goat cheese or Montrachet)

3 large eggs

1 cup sour cream

7 chives, finely chopped

2 teaspoons pepper

1 recipe Savory Tart Dough (p. 10), fully baked in either individual tartlets or one large tart

PREHEAT THE OVEN TO 375°F.

In a medium sauté pan, heat the olive oil. Add the onions to the pan, and sprinkle them with the salt. At medium-low heat, gently caramelize the onions. They should turn a light golden brown.

Place the goat cheese in a bowl, and soften with a spoon. Gradually incorporate the eggs. When the eggs have been completely incorporated, mix in the sour cream. Season the filling with fresh pepper and chives. Goat cheese is usually a little salty, so check for salt before adding more.

Arrange the tart shells on a sheet tray, and divide the caramelized onions between them. Place the tray in a preheated oven, and pour the cheese mixture over the onions. Fill the tarts up to the top with the goat cheese mixture.

Bake the tarts at 375°F for 20 to 30 minutes or until the centers appear set.

notes

almonds: Almond Coconut Crumble, 28; Apricot Frangipane Tart, 93; Cranberry Almond Tart, 101

Amish Vanilla Pie, 49

apples: Apple Cranberry Brown Betty, 27; Apple Turnovers, 81; Farm Stand Apple Pie, 15–16; Handkerchief Apple Pie, 84–85; Pennsylvania Dutch Apple Dumplings, 76–77

apricots: Apricot Frangipane Tart, 93; Individual Apricot Cherry Fried Pies, 78–79

bacon: Quiche Lorraine, 111

bananas: Caramelized Banana Cream Pie, 36–37

berries: Apple Cranberry Brown Betty, 27; Cranberry Almond Tart, 101; French Silk Pie with Raspberries, 62; Fresh Berry Tart, 99–100; Frozen Strawberry Cloud Pie, 29; Mixed Berry Turnovers, 80–81; Nectarine Blueberry Crisp, 86–87; Raspberry Custard Pie, 24–25; Raspberry Jam Tart, 96–97; Raspberry Sauce, 97; Rhubarb Strawberry Pie, 22–23; True Blueberry Pie, 17–18

Black Bottom Chiffon Pie, 63–64

blueberries. *See* berries

Bourbon Pecan Pie, 33–34

caramel: Caramel Sauce, 61; Coconut-and-Rum Caramel Sauce, 35; Walnut Caramel Tart, 94–95

Caramelized Banana Cream Pie, 36–37

Cheddar Cheese Corn Pie, 112

cheese: Cheddar Cheese Corn Pie, 112; Onion Goat Cheese Tart, 115; Quiche Lorraine, 111; Spinach Feta Pie, 109–10. *See also* cheesecakes

cheesecakes: Chocolate Cream Cheese Peaks, 60–61; Pumpkin Cheesecake Pie, 43–44

cherries: Bourbon Pecan Pie, 33–34; Clafoutis Cherry Custard Tart, 98; Deep-Dish Sour Cherry Pie, 19; Individual Apricot Cherry Fried Pies, 78–79

chess pies: Chocolate Lemon Chess Pie, 57–58; Pineapple Chess Pie, 41–42

chocolate, 54; Black Bottom Chiffon Pie, 63–64; Bourbon Pecan Pie, 33–34; Chocolate Candy Bar Pie, 55–56; Chocolate Cream Cheese Peaks, 60–61; Chocolate Fudge

Topping, 66–67; Chocolate Lemon Chess Pie, 57–58; Chocolate Whipped Cream, 95; Double Chocolate Ganache Tarts, 105; French Silk Pie with Raspberries, 62; Frozen Peanut Butter Mousse Pie, 65; Fudge Brownie Pie, 59; Mini Molten Pies, 68–69; Mississippi Mud Ice Cream Pie, 67
Clafoutis Cherry Custard Tart, 98
coconut: Almond Coconut Crumble, 28; Coconut-and-Rum Caramel Sauce, 35; Toasted Coconut Custard Pie, 35
Coconut-and-Rum Caramel Sauce, 35
Cookie Crust, 7
corn: Cheddar Cheese Corn Pie, 112
cranberries. *See* berries
Cranberry Almond Tart, 101
Cream Cheese Pie Dough, 6
crusts, 2–3, 11; Cookie Crust, 7; Cream Cheese Pie Dough, 6; Heirloom Pie Dough, 5; No-Roll Pie Dough, 9; Perfect Pie Dough, 4–5; Savory Tart Dough, 10; Sweet Tart Dough, 8
custard: Black Bottom Chiffon Pie, 63–64; Clafoutis Cherry Custard Tart, 98; Raspberry Custard Pie, 24–25; Simple Velvet Custard Pie, 82–83; Toasted Coconut Custard Pie, 35

Deep-Dish Plum Cobbler, 88–89
Deep-Dish Sour Cherry Pie, 19
Double Chocolate Ganache Tarts, 105

dumplings: Pennsylvania Dutch Apple Dumplings, 76–77

equipment, 2–3

Farm Stand Apple Pie, 15–16
figs: Individual Fig Crostatas, 73–74
French Silk Pie with Raspberries, 62
Fresh Berry Tart, 23, 99–100
Frozen Peanut Butter Mousse Pie, 65
Frozen Strawberry Cloud Pie, 29
Fudge Brownie Pie, 59

garnishes: chocolate curls, 64; Chocolate Whipped Cream, 95; Raspberry Sauce, 97. *See also* sauces; toppings

Handkerchief Apple Pie, 84–85
Heirloom Pie Dough, 5

ice cream: Mississippi Mud Ice Cream Pie, 67
Individual Apricot Cherry Fried Pies, 78–79
Individual Fig Crostatas, 73–74

Key Lime Pie, 38

Lemon Curd Tartlets, 103–4
lemons: Chocolate Lemon Chess Pie, 57–58; Lemon Curd Tartlets, 103–4; Mile-High Lemon Meringue Pie, 39–40

Lime Daiquiri Chiffon Pie, 47–48
limes: Key Lime Pie, 38; Lime Daiquiri
    Chiffon Pie, 47–48

meats: Steak and Kidney Pie, 113–14
meringue: Caramelized Banana Cream
    Pie, 36–37; Mile-High Lemon
    Meringue Pie, 39–40; Sour Cream
    Raisin Pie, 50–51
Mile-High Lemon Meringue Pie, 39–40
mincemeat, 102
Mini Molten Pies, 68–69
Mississippi Mud Ice Cream Pie, 67
Mixed Berry Turnovers, 80–81
molasses: Amish Vanilla Pie, 49

Nectarine Blueberry Crisp, 86–87
No-Roll Pie Dough, 9

oatmeal: Pear Raisin Oatmeal Crisp, 26
Onion Goat Cheese Tart, 115

pastry cream (for tarts), 99–100
peaches: Prize-Winning Peach Pie, 20–21
peanut butter: Frozen Peanut Butter
    Mousse Pie, 65
Pear Galette, 75
Pear Raisin Oatmeal Crisp, 26
pears: Pear Galette, 75; Pear Raisin
    Oatmeal Crisp, 26
pecans: Bourbon Pecan Pie, 33–34;
    Southern Sweet Potato Pie, 45–46

Pennsylvania Dutch Apple Dumplings,
    76–77
Perfect Pie Dough, 4–5
pie crust. *See* crusts
Pineapple Chess Pie, 41–42
plums: Deep-Dish Plum Cobbler, 88–89
Prize-Winning Peach Pie, 20–21
Pumpkin Cheesecake Pie, 43–44

Quiche Lorraine, 111

raisins: Bourbon Pecan Pie, 33–34; Pear
    Raisin Oatmeal Crisp, 26; Sour Cream
    Raisin Pie, 50–51
raspberries. *See* berries
Raspberry Custard Pie, 24–25
Raspberry Jam Tart, 96–97
Raspberry Sauce, 97
Rhubarb Strawberry Pie, 22–23
rum: Coconut-and-Rum Caramel Sauce,
    35; Lime Daiquiri Chiffon Pie, 47–48

sauces: Caramel Sauce, 61; Chocolate
    Fudge Topping, 66; Coconut-and-Rum
    Caramel Sauce, 35. *See also* garnishes;
    toppings
Savory Tart Dough, 10
Simple Velvet Custard Pie, 82–83
Sour Cream Raisin Pie, 50–51
Southern Sweet Potato Pie, 45–46
spinach: Quiche Lorraine, 111; Spinach
    Feta Pie, 109–10

Spinach Feta Pie, 109–10
Steak and Kidney Pie, 113–14
strawberries. *See* berries
sweet potatoes: Southern Sweet Potato
  Pie, 45–46
Sweet Tart Dough, 8

tart crust. *See* crusts
Toasted Coconut Custard Pie, 35

toppings: Almond Coconut Crumble, 28;
  Amish Crumb Topping, 49. *See also*
  garnishes; sauces
True Blueberry Pie, 17–18

vanilla: Amish Vanilla Pie, 49; Black
  Bottom Chiffon Pie, 63–64

Walnut Caramel Tart, 94–95